Babylon's Sacred
Rituals of

Babylon's Sacred Magic: Spells, Sigils, and Rituals of the Ancient World

COPYRIGHT

All rights reserved. No part of this guide may be reproduced or transmitted in any form or by any means, electronic or mechanical, including photocopying, recording, or by any information storage and retrieval system, without written permission from the publisher.

This is a work of creative fiction. Some parts have been fictionalized in varying degrees for various purposes.

Copyright © **AD Publishing**, 2024

All rights reserved. No part of this book may be reproduced in any form by any electronic or mechanical means, including information storage and retrieval systems, without permission in writing from the publisher, except by a reviewer who may quote brief passages in a review.

ISBN 9798306830537

COPYRIGHT

DISCLAIMER

This guide is intended for information and educational purposes only. In no event shall its authors, publishers, suppliers or partners be liable for any damages (including without limitation, damages for loss of data or profit, or due to business interruption) arising out of the use or inability to use the materials in this guide. Readers are advised to conduct their own research and due diligence and consult with a qualified professional before making any purchasing or financial decisions.

DISCLOSURE

This electronic version of this book may include hyperlinks to products and learning resources for reader convenience. The authors participate in various affiliate programs which may cover some of the tools and resources mentioned in this guide. This means they may earn a nominal fee on purchases from related partner websites.

Table Of Contents

Contents

Babylon's Sacred Magic: Spells, Sigils, and Rituals of the Ancient World 1

COPYRIGHT 3

DISCLAIMER 5

DISCLOSURE 6

Table Of Contents 7

Introduction 10

Chapter 1: The Cursed Seals of Enlil 14

Chapter 2: The Rituals of Binding and the Price of Power 19

Chapter 3: The Sacred Sigils and the Language of the Eternal 25

Chapter 4: The Rites of Summoning and the Bonding of the Unseen 32

Chapter 5: The Enchantment of Seals and the Locks of Power 39

Chapter 6: The Spirits of the Seals and the Veiled Pact 47

Chapter 6: The Forbidden Grimoire and the Whispering Shadows 54

Table Of Contents

Chapter 7: The Veil Between Worlds and the Path of Crossing 62

Chapter 8: The Song of the Elements and the Binding of Forces 70

Chapter 9: The Shadows of Creation and the Forgotten Craft 79

Chapter 10: The Gates of the Stars and the Forbidden Ascent 87

Chapter 12: The Veil of Dreams and the Path of Night's Whisper 105

Chapter 13: The Codex of Whispers and the Secrets of Hidden Tongues 114

Chapter 14: The Incantations of Akkadia: Spells of Power, Protection, and Transformation 122

Chapter 15: The Incantations of Babylon: Spells of Dominion, Healing, and the Stars 130

Chapter 16: The Incantations of Sumer: Spells of Creation, Balance, and the Divine 139

Appendix: Glossary and Ritual Compendium 147

Table Of Contents

Introduction

Lo, beware, dear reader, for thou art poised to embark upon a perilous journey into the eldritch annals of sorcery most ancient, where mortal man doth tread only at the peril of his immortal soul. The words herein do whisper of Babylon, that cursed and hallowed citelecy of antiquity, whose very name doth tremble upon the lips of the wise and conjure dread in the hearts of the devout. For in its shadowed streets and smoke-suffused temples did magicians and priests conspire with forces unseen, bending the very threads of the cosmos to their will.

These pages, penned with trembling hand, do reveal the spells and rites of Babylon's magi—practices wrought from the bones of gods and the sighs of stars. But take heed, for knowledge is oft a double-edged blade, and herein lies not only the power to protect but the peril of perdition. To speak the names of their forgotten gods, to inscribe their sigils upon clay, is to summon forth powers long banished to the yawning void of the outer

Introduction

realms. Their seals, etched with cuneiform runes, are the locks to gateways best left closed, and their rituals, once performed, do echo in realms far beyond the ken of mortal reckoning.

In Babylon, the rivers ran thick with secrets, their currents laden with the whispers of Enki, the god of wisdom and mischief. The moon, pale and watchful, cast its gaze upon rituals performed beneath its unblinking eye. And in the shadow of the Ziggurats, whose steps rose like a stairway to the heavens, the priests of Marduk called forth the winds of creation and destruction alike. It is said that their incantations could command the storm to lie still or summon it to lay waste to the mightiest city. What then, might such magic do to a lone soul who dares to wield it?

Oh, foolish seeker, dost thou not hear the cries of those who have ventured too far into such forbidden realms? Their voices are but echoes now, lost in the winds of eternity, their eyes forever cast into the void. Yet still, thou persist, compelled by the hunger that gnaws at

Introduction

the core of thy spirit—a hunger for power, for knowledge, for a touch of that which lies beyond the veil.

Gaze not too long into the glyphs and symbols of these ancient spells, for they are not merely marks upon clay but keys to forces older than the earth beneath thy feet. The stars themselves have watched as these rites were performed—stars that burn with an eternal fire and weep tears of light for the folly of men. Their light hath borne witness to the summoning of spirits unbridled, whose forms do shimmer like smoke and whose voices are a chorus of sighs and screams.

Thus, I do write these words not as a guide but as a warning—a grim testament to the dangers of the craft thou art so eager to embrace. The seals of Babylon are not mere trinkets but talismans of power wrought in the crucible of divine wrath and human ambition. To grasp them is to seize a serpent by its tail, its fangs poised to strike at the very marrow of thy being.

Introduction

And yet, if thou art resolved—if no entreaty of mine can stay thy hand—then proceed, but with caution etched into thy heart. Call upon the gods of old with reverence and fear, for their gaze is heavy, and their patience is thin. Prepare thyself for the darkling paths ahead, where shadows shift and whisper, and the air itself doth tremble with a thousand unseen wings.

May the divine grant thee wisdom, and may thy soul emerge unscathed from the labyrinth of Babylonian sorcery. For thou art about to walk in the footsteps of gods and demons alike, and the echoes of thy journey may well reverberate through eternity.

Chapter 1: The Cursed Seals of Enlil

In the desolate winds that sweep across the barren plains, where the stars weep in silence and the moon bears witness to secrets older than the earth itself, there lies a tale of power so dark and consuming that even the gods dared not speak its name. The Seals of Enlil, forged in the breath of the heavens and tempered in the fires of divine wrath, are relics of a forgotten time, when men sought to wield the forces of creation and chaos as their own.

These seals, inscribed upon clay tablets with glyphs that twist and writhe as if alive, are no mere tools of magic but locks to the primal energies that pulse through the veins of existence. They are the breath of storms, the cries of winds that lash at mountains, and the sighs of the earth as it groans beneath the weight of eternity. To behold a seal is to gaze upon a fragment of the divine—its edges sharp with the promise of power and the curse of ruin.

Chapter 1: The Cursed Seals of Enlil

It is whispered that Enlil, the lord of storms and the wrathful god of the heavens, did craft these seals to bind the spirits of chaos and keep the balance of the cosmos intact. But the hands of mortals, ever grasping and insatiable, sought to claim them for their own. For what is man if not a creature of ambition, eager to command the forces that shape his world? And so, the seals fell into the hands of those bold enough—or foolish enough—to believe they could wield the will of the heavens.

The Seal of the Thunderous Breath

The first of these seals is said to hold the voice of Enlil himself, a thunderous roar that can tear asunder the foundations of mountains and scatter armies as leaves before a gale. To invoke this seal is to summon the storm, to command the winds to rise and the heavens to weep with rain and lightning. But beware, for the storm answers to no master and heeds no plea for mercy. Many a sorcerer who dared to speak its incantation has been consumed by the very tempest they sought to unleash.

Chapter 1: The Cursed Seals of Enlil

The ritual is a harrowing one, requiring the blood of a lamb offered beneath an open sky, where the stars gaze down with cold indifference. The incantation, written in the ancient tongue of the gods, must be spoken with a voice steady as the earth itself, lest the storm turn upon its summoner. The seal must be drawn upon a tablet of purest clay, its glyphs carved with the precision of a surgeon's blade, each line a conduit for the power it contains.

The Seal of Whispering Shadows

The second seal is a thing of subtlety and dread, for it holds the power to command the shadows themselves. To invoke this seal is to summon spirits unseen, whose forms shift and flicker like smoke caught in the moonlight. These spirits are the messengers of the underworld, their voices a chorus of whispers that speak of truths hidden and secrets buried.

Yet, to command the shadows is to tread a perilous path, for they are not creatures of loyalty but entities of chaos and deceit. The

Chapter 1: The Cursed Seals of Enlil

seal must be crafted in utter darkness, its glyphs inscribed with ink blacker than the void, and its ritual performed beneath the waning moon, when its light is weakest. The sorcerer must offer a fragment of their own shadow, a piece of their soul bound to the seal, as the price for its power.

The Seal of the Boundless Void

Most feared of all is the third seal, said to hold the very essence of the void—the space between worlds where time ceases to flow and light dares not tread. To invoke this seal is to open a gateway to the beyond, to summon forth the primordial chaos from which all things were born and to which all things shall return.

The ritual is a thing of horror, requiring the ashes of a burned star sigil and the sacrifice of one's deepest fear. The seal must be inscribed upon obsidian, its glyphs etched with a blade forged from meteorite. To complete the ritual is to risk one's very existence, for the void is not merely a place but a force that consumes all who gaze too deeply into its abyss.

Chapter 1: The Cursed Seals of Enlil

The Consequences of Power

The Seals of Enlil are not to be wielded lightly, for their power is a double-edged sword, and their price is always greater than it seems. Those who dare to summon the storm, to command the shadows, or to open the void must be prepared to face the consequences of their ambition. For the seals do not grant power; they lend it, and their debt must always be paid.

And so, as you stand upon the threshold of this forbidden knowledge, take heed of the warnings that echo through the ages. The seals are a gift and a curse, a bridge to the divine and a pathway to damnation. To wield them is to walk in the footsteps of gods and to risk the wrath of the heavens themselves. Choose wisely, for the seals hold not only the power to shape your destiny but the power to unmake it.

Chapter 2: The Rituals of Binding and the Price of Power

In the still of the night, when the air is thick with silence and the stars burn with cold fire, the rituals of binding take shape. These ancient ceremonies, known to but a few and whispered of in trembling voices, are the keys to unlocking the seals of Mesopotamia. Yet, the price they demand is steep, for they tether the sorcerer's very soul to the realms of gods and shadows.

The rituals are not mere incantations but acts of will, performed in the liminal spaces where the mortal and the divine collide. They require offerings of blood and breath, the essence of life itself, for the seals are not to be trifled with. Each ritual is a gateway, a pact struck with forces beyond comprehension, and each carries its own peril.

The Rite of the Crescent Flame

The first of these rituals is the Rite of the Crescent Flame, performed beneath a crescent moon that bathes the earth in its pale, ghostly

Chapter 2: The Rituals of Binding and the Price of Power

glow. It is a ceremony of fire and sacrifice, calling upon the power of Enlil's wrath to scorch the earth and cleanse the spirit.

The sorcerer must prepare a sacred flame, kindled with wood from a tree struck by lightning and anointed with oil pressed from the seeds of the black lotus. The flame must burn upon an altar carved with the glyphs of the storm, and its light must touch neither shadow nor darkness. Into the flame, the sorcerer must cast an offering—an object imbued with their deepest fear, a fragment of their own mortality. The incantation, spoken in the language of the gods, must rise like smoke into the heavens, a prayer and a plea entwined.

But beware, for the flame is a living thing, hungry and unyielding. Should the sorcerer falter or stray from the path, the flame will consume more than the offering. It will devour the soul of the unworthy, leaving behind naught but ash and regret.

The Dance of the Shadowed Veil

Chapter 2: The Rituals of Binding and the Price of Power

The second ritual is a thing of beauty and terror, a dance performed in the light of the waning moon. It is said that the veil between worlds grows thin in these hours, and the shadows gather to witness the sorcerer's descent into their realm.

The sorcerer must don a robe of black silk, its threads spun from the webs of nocturnal spiders and dyed with the ink of the squid. Upon their brow must rest a circlet of onyx, a crown to mark them as sovereign of the shadows. The ritual begins with a single step, a movement that sets the rhythm of the dance. With each step, the sorcerer must speak the names of the shadow spirits, calling them forth to bear witness.

The dance is both a summoning and a test, for the shadows are cunning and cruel. They will offer the sorcerer visions of power and glory, temptations to lead them astray. Only those with unwavering will can complete the dance, binding the shadows to their command without succumbing to their whispers.

The Sacrament of the Celestial Tear

Chapter 2: The Rituals of Binding and the Price of Power

Most dangerous of all is the Sacrament of the Celestial Tear, a ritual said to draw power from the stars themselves. It requires the sorcerer to capture the essence of a falling star, a fragment of the heavens brought down to earth.

The ritual begins with a journey to a sacred place, a site where the earth and sky meet in harmony. There, beneath the open heavens, the sorcerer must craft a vessel to hold the star's essence. The vessel must be forged from meteoric iron and inscribed with the seals of the cosmos, each glyph a conduit for the power it contains.

When the star falls, its light must be caught within the vessel, a feat requiring perfect timing and unwavering focus. The sorcerer must then perform the incantation, a hymn to the stars written in the language of the ancients. As the light of the star fills the vessel, the sorcerer will feel its power coursing through their veins, a sensation both intoxicating and terrifying.

Chapter 2: The Rituals of Binding and the Price of Power

But the stars are not generous. They do not give their power freely, and the sorcerer must offer something in return. The price is always personal—a memory, a hope, a piece of their very being. To take the power of the stars is to give up a part of oneself, a sacrifice that cannot be undone.

The Perils of Binding

To complete a ritual is to gain power, but it is also to take on a burden. The seals and their rituals are not tools to be used lightly but bonds that tie the sorcerer to forces beyond their control. The power they grant is fleeting, and the price they demand is eternal.

The ancients knew this truth, and they feared the seals as much as they revered them. For every sorcerer who succeeded in binding their power, there were countless others who fell, consumed by the very forces they sought to command. The seals are not kind, and their power is not merciful. They are a mirror, reflecting the sorcerer's soul and magnifying their flaws.

Chapter 2: The Rituals of Binding and the Price of Power

And so, as you prepare to embark upon the path of the seals, remember this: the rituals are not merely acts of magic but acts of sacrifice. They are a test of will, a trial of the soul. To bind the seals is to walk a path of power and peril, a journey that will shape your destiny and define your fate. Choose wisely, for the seals will take as much as they give, and their price is one that must always be paid.

Chapter 3: The Sacred Sigils and the Language of the Eternal

Oh, wanderer of perilous ambition, take heed, for you tread now upon the hallowed ground of the sigils—the timeless marks that speak the language of gods and forgotten realms. These sacred designs, etched in the veins of Mesopotamian magic, are not mere symbols but living vessels of power, tethered to the heavens, the earth, and the underworld. They are the whispers of immortals and the echoes of creation, wielded by mortals at great peril and immeasurable cost.

To inscribe a sigil is to carve a piece of eternity, to draw forth the will of the cosmos and bind it to the fragile vessel of flesh. But be warned, seeker, for each line, each curve, is a thread in a tapestry beyond mortal comprehension. To err is to invite ruin; to falter is to summon wrath.

Chapter 3: The Sacred Sigils and the Language of the Eternal

The Birth of the Sigils

It is said that the first sigils were gifted to mortals by Enki, the keeper of wisdom, who saw fit to bestow fragments of divine power upon humanity. These markings, intricate and infinite in meaning, served as conduits between the realms of the living and the immortal. They were not written but born, shaped by the stars themselves and imbued with the essence of the gods.

In the tablets of clay and the carvings of stone, these sigils have endured. They are found upon the seals of kings, the doorways of temples, and the amulets of the wise. Each sigil carries a story, a purpose, and a power, yet their true meaning remains veiled, known only to the brave—or the foolish—who dare to wield them.

The Sigils of Power

Among the sigils, there are those that call forth strength, drawing upon the boundless energy of the divine. These are the Sigils of

Chapter 3: The Sacred Sigils and the Language of the Eternal

Power, etched in spirals of force and marked with the glyphs of the elements.

To craft such a sigil, one must gather the tools of the ancients: a quill fashioned from the feather of a raven, ink mixed with ash from a sacred flame, and a parchment made from the skin of a beast felled beneath the full moon. The sigil must be drawn in a single, unbroken motion, for hesitation severs the flow of power, leaving only an empty husk.

The incantation, spoken with breath drawn from the depths of the soul, awakens the sigil, binding its energy to the sorcerer. Yet the power is not given freely. The Sigils of Power demand balance, taking from the sorcerer as much as they give. To use them is to risk the erosion of one's own essence, a toll paid in strength, vitality, or even the fading of memory.

The Sigils of Protection

In times of great peril, when the shadows grow long and the breath of demons stirs the

Chapter 3: The Sacred Sigils and the Language of the Eternal

air, the Sigils of Protection stand as bastions against the abyss. These sigils, wrought with lines of fire and circles of stone, are shields against the unseen forces that hunger for mortal souls.

To inscribe a Sigil of Protection, the sorcerer must seek a place of stillness, where the wind carries no sound and the earth sleeps beneath the stars. The sigil must be drawn upon a surface of unbroken purity—be it a circle of salt, a tablet of ivory, or a mirror of obsidian. Each stroke must be made with intent, for the sigil reflects the heart of its maker. To inscribe with doubt is to leave the gate ajar, inviting the very forces one seeks to repel.

The invocation that binds the sigil is a hymn to the gods of order, a plea for their guardianship. As the words rise into the night, the sigil awakens, a barrier of light and shadow that stands between the sorcerer and the void. But beware, for the sigil is only as strong as the will that created it. To falter is to fail, and to fail is to fall into the abyss.

Chapter 3: The Sacred Sigils and the Language of the Eternal

The Sigils of Passage

Rarest and most perilous of all are the Sigils of Passage, marks that open the gates between realms. These sigils, forbidden to all but the most daring, are keys to the unseen worlds where gods and spirits dwell. They are the bridges between the known and the unknowable, paths that few have walked and fewer have returned from.

To craft a Sigil of Passage, the sorcerer must first seek the favor of the spirits, offering gifts of rare incense, unblemished pearls, and songs sung in the forgotten tongues of the ancients. The sigil, once inscribed, becomes a door—a portal that trembles with the breath of otherworldly winds.

The passage is not without its trials. To step through the gate is to leave behind the safety of the mortal realm and to walk in the shadow of gods. The traveler must carry tokens of grounding—stones from the river's edge, threads of silver bound to their wrist—to anchor their spirit lest they be lost in the currents of eternity. And always, the sigil must

Chapter 3: The Sacred Sigils and the Language of the Eternal

remain intact, for a broken sigil is a shattered bridge, stranding the traveler in realms unknown.

The Perils of the Sigils

Oh, ye who seek the sigils, know this: they are not tools but living forces, bound to the will of the gods and the laws of the cosmos. To wield them is to invite their gaze, and their gaze is neither kind nor forgiving.

The sigils do not bend to mortals; they demand reverence, precision, and sacrifice. To misuse a sigil is to unweave the threads of fate, unraveling the delicate balance of the universe. And yet, for those who master them, the sigils offer power beyond measure, a glimpse of the eternal, and a bond with the divine.

But tread carefully, for the path of the sigils is narrow and treacherous, a road paved with the ashes of those who have fallen. Remember, seeker, the sigils do not choose

Chapter 3: The Sacred Sigils and the Language of the Eternal

the worthy. They test the willing, and their judgment is final.

Chapter 4: The Rites of Summoning and the Bonding of the Unseen

Oh, trembling soul, whose shadow now falls upon the precipice of forbidden arts, know that the rites of summoning are not for the faint of heart or the timid of will. They are the oldest of magics, whispered before the dawn of kings, when the heavens were closer, and the earth groaned with the weight of gods walking among men. To summon is to beckon the unseen, to stir the slumbering forces that lie dormant between the cracks of the mortal world. Yet, such a call is neither simple nor safe—it is a pact of blood and breath, of intention and sacrifice.

The Nature of Summoning

To summon is not merely to call; it is to forge a bridge between realms, to extend a hand into the unknown and hope it is not seized by

Chapter 4: The Rites of Summoning and the Bonding of the Unseen

something beyond reckoning. The ancient magicians of Babylon, who dared to inscribe their will upon the fabric of the cosmos, understood this peril. They knew that the beings summoned—whether spirits of the earth, the heavens, or the netherworld—were not servants but entities of immense power, bound by rules older than the stars themselves.

These rites demand absolute precision, for the slightest misstep can tear the veil between worlds, unleashing chaos upon both summoner and land. The symbols must be drawn with unwavering hand, the incantations uttered with flawless breath, and the offerings given with a heart free of doubt. For in the presence of these beings, the mortal soul is but a flickering candle in a tempest.

The Circle of Dominion

At the heart of every summoning lies the circle of dominion, a sacred space that serves as both shield and vessel. It is within this boundary that the summoned entity must

Chapter 4: The Rites of Summoning and the Bonding of the Unseen

appear, bound to its confines by the force of the summoner's will. The circle is not merely drawn but birthed through ritual, inscribed with sigils of containment, protection, and power.

The materials for crafting the circle are as vital as the rites themselves. Salt from the deepest seas, chalk ground from sacred stones, and ashes of herbs burned under the light of the waxing moon—these are but the foundation. The circle must be adorned with runes of precision, each line and curve imbued with the essence of the summoner's intent.

Once drawn, the summoner must step within, becoming one with the circle, a sentinel at its heart. To step outside is to relinquish control, to invite the entity into the mortal realm without barrier or bond. Within the circle, the summoner is both master and mediator, standing at the threshold of two worlds.

The Call to the Unseen

Chapter 4: The Rites of Summoning and the Bonding of the Unseen

The act of summoning begins with the invocation, a chant that reaches beyond the mortal tongue into the language of the unseen. These words, passed down through generations of magicians, carry the weight of ages, their syllables vibrating with the resonance of creation itself.

Each entity has its own call, its own key to the lock of its realm. To summon the spirits of the earth, one must speak in tones that mimic the rumble of stone and the sigh of wind through ancient trees. For the beings of the heavens, the voice must rise like the song of the stars, clear and unwavering. And for those of the netherworld, the words must carry the weight of shadow, whispered with breath drawn from the depths of the soul.

The offering, too, is essential. Honey and wine for spirits of abundance, rare gems for those of the celestial spheres, and blood—be it animal or the summoner's own—for the denizens of the abyss. These offerings are not mere gifts but tokens of trust, proof that the summoner is worthy of the entity's presence.

Chapter 4: The Rites of Summoning and the Bonding of the Unseen

---

The Binding and the Bargain

Once the entity appears, shimmering at the edge of sight or roaring into form, the summoner must enact the binding—a rite that secures the entity within the circle and seals its power to the summoner's will. This is a moment of peril, for the entity will test the summoner's resolve, probing for weakness, seeking cracks in the armor of intent.

The binding is not an act of force but a negotiation, a delicate dance of power and persuasion. The summoner must declare their purpose with clarity, for the entity is bound only by agreements willingly made. Yet these beings are cunning, their wisdom spanning millennia. They will seek to twist words, to find loopholes, to extract a price far greater than the summoner intends to pay.

The terms of the bargain must be etched into the sigils of the circle, a contract sealed in the language of magic. Once agreed, the entity's power is lent to the summoner, a flame drawn from the eternal fire. Yet the bond is not

Chapter 4: The Rites of Summoning and the Bonding of the Unseen

eternal, and when the task is done, the entity must be dismissed with the same precision and respect with which it was called.

The Perils of Summoning

Oh, heed this warning, seeker of forbidden knowledge: summoning is a perilous art, fraught with risks that even the most skilled magicians cannot fully anticipate. To call forth an entity is to invite its gaze, and the gaze of the unseen is both blessing and curse.

Should the circle falter, the entity will be unleashed, free to wreak havoc upon the summoner and all who dwell nearby. Should the summoner's will waver, the bond will break, and the entity will turn upon its would-be master with wrath unbridled. And should the summoner's heart be impure, tainted by greed or malice, the entity will see it and reflect it, magnifying the summoner's flaws into ruin.

Yet for those who succeed, the rewards are beyond measure. The summoned entities hold

Chapter 4: The Rites of Summoning and the Bonding of the Unseen

secrets of creation, wisdom of the ages, and power that defies mortal comprehension. To stand in their presence is to glimpse the infinite, to touch the threads of destiny, and to wield the forces that shape the cosmos.

But remember, wanderer, the rites of summoning are not merely tools but sacred acts, bridges between the finite and the eternal. To walk this path is to dance with the gods, to court both glory and destruction. Let your heart be steady, your will unyielding, and your purpose pure, for the unseen watches, and it judges without mercy.

Chapter 5: The Enchantment of Seals and the Locks of Power

Oh, trembling wayfarer, let not thy spirit waver, for thou dost now tread upon the most sacred and perilous of the olden arts—the crafting of seals, those intricate sigils that bind the forces of the unseen to mortal will. Seals, wrought in mystery and conceived in reverence, are the locks upon the gates of arcane power, and their crafting is a journey fraught with both wonder and dread. In their curves and lines, the very language of the heavens and the netherworld is whispered, a tongue older than stone and softer than the wind that weeps through forgotten temples.

To fashion a seal is to hold in one's hands the pen of the divine scribe, to weave a spell whose echoes will resound through the corridors of eternity. Yet be warned, for the unworthy hand may twist this sacred art into folly, and the careless soul shall find ruin where it sought dominion.

Chapter 5: The Enchantment of Seals and the Locks of Power

The Origins of the Sacred Seals

In the twilight of the first age, when gods and men still spoke across the veil, it is said the seals were gifted to the ancients by the watchers of the heavens. These symbols, scrawled upon clay tablets and etched into precious metals, bore the power to summon storms, calm seas, and open gates unseen by mortal eyes. In Babylon's shadowed ziggurats, beneath the watchful gaze of the moon-god Sin, the magicians of old would carve these marks into their tools, their amulets, and their very flesh, binding themselves to the cosmic order.

Each seal is a fragment of the eternal, a reflection of the divine tapestry. They do not merely symbolize power; they are power, captured and bound in lines that curve like rivers or cut sharp like the edge of a blade.

The Tools of the Seal-Maker

Chapter 5: The Enchantment of Seals and the Locks of Power

To craft a seal is no mundane task, and the tools of the seal-maker are as sacred as the seals themselves. The stylus, often tipped with gold or obsidian, must be blessed under the light of the crescent moon. The medium—be it clay, parchment, or stone—must be prepared with rites that purify it of earthly corruption. Only those materials consecrated by fire, water, or the breath of the chanting magician are fit to bear the weight of such divine inscriptions.

The ink, a concoction steeped in mystery, is made from the ashes of burnt herbs, the blood of rare creatures, and the tears of the diligent seeker. Its consistency must be as thick as honey, for the seal must be inscribed with bold strokes, lest its power falter. The crafting of the ink is itself a ritual, performed in silence, save for the murmur of invocations to the guardians of the unseen.

The Ritual of Creation

Before the seal-maker sets hand to work, a sacred circle must be drawn, inscribed with

Chapter 5: The Enchantment of Seals and the Locks of Power

protective glyphs to guard against the energies unleashed by the crafting. A brazier of smoldering incense fills the air with a haze thick with the scent of myrrh and cedar, the smoke rising like tendrils of forgotten spirits.

The seal is not drawn; it is summoned. The maker's hand, guided by whispers and visions, must move with precision, for every line and curve holds meaning. A single stroke too wide, a single mark out of place, and the seal's purpose shall twist, becoming a beacon for chaos rather than order.

As the seal takes form, the maker must chant, the words rising and falling like the tide. These chants are not mere sounds but keys, unlocking the hidden potential of the seal. The words must flow with the rhythm of the cosmos, for the seal is not merely a creation but a bridge, binding the will of the maker to the forces of the eternal.

The Power Bound Within

Chapter 5: The Enchantment of Seals and the Locks of Power

Each seal is a vessel, a prison for power that would otherwise roam untamed. The magicians of Babylon, who first mastered this art, understood that each seal held a specific resonance, attuned to the forces it was meant to command. Some seals call forth the winds, bidding them to carry messages across the desert sands. Others bind spirits of flame, their heat a servant to the magician's will. And there are those seals, darker and more forbidden, which open doorways to the netherworld, summoning beings whose names are best left unspoken.

Once crafted, the seal must be consecrated. This is the moment of binding, when the maker calls upon the forces to inhabit the seal. The brazier's flames roar higher as the seal is passed through smoke, fire, or water, each element imbuing it with its own essence. The seal is then anointed with oil or blood, the final act of dedication.

The Usage of Seals

Chapter 5: The Enchantment of Seals and the Locks of Power

The completed seal is no idle trinket. It is an instrument of great power, a key to realms unseen. To use a seal is to unleash the forces bound within, directing them with the authority of the maker's will. Yet, this power must be wielded with care, for the forces contained in the seal are neither benevolent nor malevolent—they are, simply, power.

The seal must be held aloft, its glyphs facing the heavens, as the maker speaks the command. The words must match the resonance of the seal, for it is through this harmony that the forces are directed. A seal of protection, for instance, must be activated with words of shielding and light, while a seal of summoning demands invocations that call forth the entity it binds.

But be warned, for the seal's power is not infinite. Each use drains its essence, and should it be overused, it shall crumble, releasing its forces unchecked. And should the seal be shattered by violence or neglect, its energies shall recoil upon the maker with a wrath that no mortal can withstand.

Chapter 5: The Enchantment of Seals and the Locks of Power

The Dangers of Seals

Oh, seeker of power, know this: the crafting of seals is a path fraught with peril. To inscribe a seal is to channel the forces of the cosmos, and the cosmos does not take kindly to those who would bend its will without reverence. The unprepared hand shall find its seals turned against it, their energies lashing out like serpents disturbed in their lair.

And beware the seals of old, those ancient marks left by magicians long dead. These seals, faded and cracked, still hold their power, but it is twisted by time and decay. To use such a seal is to gamble with forces that even the ancients feared.

Yet, for those with the skill and the will, the seals offer a glimpse of the divine. They are the handwriting of the gods, the locks and keys to the mysteries of existence. To craft and use them is to step into a role both humble and exalted, to become a steward of forces far beyond mortal comprehension.

Chapter 5: The Enchantment of Seals and the Locks of Power

So take up thy stylus, trembling seeker, and let the ink flow like the rivers of Babylon. Let thy lines carve the fabric of reality, and let thy chants echo through the halls of eternity. For in the seals lies the power to shape the world, to command the elements, and to touch the very face of the divine. But tread lightly, for the forces thou dost summon are as ancient as the stars, and as unforgiving as the sands of time.

Chapter 6: The Spirits of the Seals and the Veiled Pact

Oh, daring wanderer, thou art come now to the most treacherous threshold of the arcane arts—the summoning of spirits bound to the sacred seals. These ethereal beings, born of realms unseen and powers unmeasured, are the breath of the seals made manifest, their will entwined with the ancient glyphs. To summon such spirits is not merely an act of magic but a dance upon the edge of existence, where one misstep may cast thee into shadow eternal.

The spirits of the seals are neither friend nor foe; they are the keepers of the seals' power, guardians of the gates they unlock, and vessels of wisdom beyond mortal grasp. Yet, they are capricious as the wind and perilous as the sea. To call upon them is to enter into a pact, a bond forged in the fires of intention and sealed with the weight of thy soul.

The Nature of the Spirits

Chapter 6: The Spirits of the Seals and the Veiled Pact

The spirits bound to the seals are creatures of paradox, both infinite in their wisdom and narrow in their purpose. Each spirit is a fragment of the greater cosmos, a shard of divine will, and yet, within their essence lies an autonomy that defies mortal comprehension. They are messengers of the gods, servants of the eternal forces, and reflections of the summoner's intent.

These spirits are as varied as the seals themselves. Some are beings of light, their forms radiant and their voices like the chiming of distant bells. Others are shadowed and formless, their presence felt as a chill upon the skin or a whisper at the edge of hearing. And then there are those who defy all understanding, their appearances shifting like smoke, their voices a cacophony of truths and half-truths.

The Summoning Ritual

To summon a spirit is to invoke the essence of the seal to which it is bound. The ritual is one of precision and reverence, for the spirits

Chapter 6: The Spirits of the Seals and the Veiled Pact

brook no error and suffer no disrespect. The summoner must prepare a sacred space, a circle drawn with care and adorned with the symbols of protection and binding.

The materials of the ritual are as vital as the words themselves. A chalice of purest silver, filled with water drawn under the light of the waning moon, serves as a mirror to reflect the spirit's form. Candles, crafted from beeswax and anointed with oils of frankincense and myrrh, provide the light that calls the spirit forth. And incense, burned in a brazier of iron, carries the summoner's intent upon its smoke.

The invocation must be spoken in the tongue of the ancients, its syllables resonating with the frequency of the seal. Each word is a key, each phrase a lock undone, and as the summoner speaks, the air grows heavy, charged with the presence of the unseen. When the final word is spoken, the spirit appears, its form shimmering within the circle, its voice echoing in the stillness.

Chapter 6: The Spirits of the Seals and the Veiled Pact

The Pact of the Spirit

The summoning is but the first step, for the spirit will not act without a pact. This agreement, forged in the moment of meeting, binds the spirit's power to the summoner's will. Yet, the terms of the pact must be chosen with care, for the spirits are cunning and their bargains are rarely as they seem.

The summoner must state their intent clearly, their voice steady and their purpose unwavering. Whether it is knowledge sought, a task performed, or a boon granted, the request must be within the spirit's domain. To ask the wrong thing is to court disaster, for the spirits cannot grant what lies beyond their power, and their wrath at such folly is swift.

The spirit will name its price, a sacrifice that must be given in exchange for its aid. This price is always personal—a memory, a fragment of the soul, a vow that binds the summoner's fate to the spirit's own. To refuse the price is to end the pact, and the spirit will depart, leaving behind only the echo of its presence.

Chapter 6: The Spirits of the Seals and the Veiled Pact

The Binding of the Spirit

Once the pact is made, the spirit must be bound to the seal, its power locked within the glyphs that called it forth. This binding is a delicate process, for the spirit will resist, testing the summoner's resolve and seeking any flaw in their intention.

The seal, inscribed upon clay or stone, must be anointed with the spirit's essence—be it a drop of its light, a whisper of its breath, or a shadow cast by its form. The summoner must then speak the binding words, their voice rising and falling like the tide, until the spirit's power flows into the seal.

As the binding is completed, the seal glows with a light unseen, its glyphs pulsing with the rhythm of the spirit's presence. The summoner must then place the seal upon the altar, offering a final prayer of gratitude and respect. Only then is the spirit truly bound, its power at the summoner's command.

Chapter 6: The Spirits of the Seals and the Veiled Pact

The Dangers of the Spirits

Oh, heed this warning, seeker of the unseen: the spirits are not mere tools but beings of will and power, and to treat them as such is to invite their wrath. The circle of protection is your only barrier, a fragile line that separates thee from forces beyond comprehension. Should the circle break, the spirit will be unleashed, its vengeance swift and unrelenting.

And beware the bargains struck in haste, for the spirits are masters of deception. They will grant thy request, but their gifts often bear a hidden cost, a twist of fate that turns boon to bane. To bind a spirit is to walk a razor's edge, and the price of failure is thy very soul.

The Wisdom of the Ancients

The magicians of old, who first mastered the art of summoning, understood its peril and its promise. They knew that the spirits, though dangerous, were also gateways to knowledge and power. To call upon them was to touch

Chapter 6: The Spirits of the Seals and the Veiled Pact

the divine, to wield forces that could shape the world and alter the course of destiny.

Yet, they also knew that such power was not without cost. The spirits demand respect, their pacts require sacrifice, and their presence leaves a mark upon the summoner's soul. To summon is to take a step beyond the mortal realm, to walk in the shadow of gods and to bear the weight of their gaze.

And so, dear reader, as you stand upon the threshold of this forbidden art, remember that the spirits are not bound to serve but to test. Their power is a mirror, reflecting the truth of thy intent and the strength of thy will. If thou art found wanting, the spirits will show no mercy. But if thou art steadfast and pure of purpose, they may yet grant thee the power to shape the cosmos itself.

Chapter 6: The Forbidden Grimoire and the Whispering Shadows

Oh, pilgrim of the arcane, thou now dost tread into the sanctum of trepidation, the realm of the forbidden grimoire, wherein the darkest secrets of Mesopotamian magic lay entombed. These are not mere tomes of parchment and ink, but vessels of power so profound that their words are said to bleed into the air when spoken, and their pages hum with the echoes of spirits long bound. To open such a book is to open the gates of shadow and light, to beckon forces both wondrous and woeful.

Yet, beware! For the grimoire is no servant to mortal will; it is a master cloaked in silence, waiting for the moment when the unwary hand shall falter. To delve into its mysteries is to wager thy very soul, to bind thy fate to the immutable laws of the unseen.

Chapter 6: The Forbidden Grimoire and the Whispering Shadows

The Origins of the Forbidden Grimoires

In the lost dawn of empires, when the gods walked the earth and whispered their secrets to mortals, the first grimoires were born. These books were not written but inscribed through rites of divine invocation, their words dictated by beings beyond comprehension. Each grimoire is said to contain not merely knowledge, but fragments of the divine essence, bound within its ink and parchment.

The grimoires of Mesopotamia are the most feared among them, their origins shrouded in myth. It is whispered that they were gifts—or perhaps curses—bestowed by the gods upon the magicians of Babylon, who sought to weave the cosmos into their grasp. Others say they were crafted by the watchers, celestial beings cast down for their defiance, who infused the books with their forbidden wisdom.

Whatever their origin, the grimoires are alive with power. Their covers are adorned with seals of protection, their pages inked with the blood of ancient beasts, and their glyphs

Chapter 6: The Forbidden Grimoire and the Whispering Shadows

shimmer with a light that no earthly flame can match. To hold such a book is to hold the weight of ages, and to read it is to unravel the very fabric of creation.

The Grimoire's Binding and Protection

No grimoire of power lies unguarded, for the words within are too potent to be left untamed. The books themselves are bound in materials as strange as their contents: leather tanned from the hides of beasts thought to be mere legend, fastened with clasps of meteoric iron and adorned with jewels that shimmer like captured starlight.

The seals upon the grimoire's cover are the first test of the seeker's resolve. These marks, inscribed by hands long turned to dust, are barriers that guard the knowledge within. To break a seal is to perform a ritual as precise as it is perilous, for each mark binds a spirit, and each spirit watches, waiting for the moment when a careless touch might unleash its wrath.

Chapter 6: The Forbidden Grimoire and the Whispering Shadows

The summoner must place the grimoire upon an altar consecrated to the gods of wisdom and shadow, surrounded by a circle of salt and flame. Only then may the seals be unbound, each one requiring an offering—a lock of hair, a drop of blood, a whispered truth too painful to bear. As the final seal is undone, the grimoire awakens, its power spilling into the air like a storm waiting to break.

The Language of the Grimoire

The words within the forbidden grimoire are no ordinary text but glyphs of divine resonance, written in the sacred tongue of the gods. To read them is not merely to see but to feel, for each symbol vibrates with an energy that resonates through the body and soul.

The language is layered, its meanings hidden within meanings, its truths obscured by riddles. A single glyph might hold the key to summoning a spirit, casting a curse, or forging a bond between realms. Yet, these truths are dangerous, for the language of the gods is not meant for mortal minds. To misread a single

Chapter 6: The Forbidden Grimoire and the Whispering Shadows

line is to invite disaster, and to understand too much is to risk madness.

The grimoire does not yield its secrets willingly. Its pages resist the touch, their edges sharp as blades, and its words shift and writhe beneath the gaze. Only those with the strength of will to command the book may hope to glean its wisdom, and even they must tread carefully, for the grimoire watches as much as it reveals.

The Spells of the Whispering Shadows

Among the countless mysteries of the grimoire, none are more feared than the spells of the whispering shadows. These incantations, said to have been gifted by the gods of the netherworld, allow the summoner to bend the forces of darkness to their will.

One such spell, the **Veil of Night**, calls forth a shadow to cloak the summoner from sight, rendering them invisible to both mortal eyes and otherworldly gaze. The ritual requires the blood of a crow, the ashes of burned

Chapter 6: The Forbidden Grimoire and the Whispering Shadows

parchment, and a chant spoken beneath a sky bereft of stars. Yet, the veil is no mere tool; it is alive, and it hungers. To use it is to feel its weight upon the soul, a constant reminder of the price of power.

Another spell, the **Binding of the Void**, allows the summoner to trap a spirit within a sigil, sealing its power for future use. The ritual demands a vessel of obsidian, an incantation sung in three voices, and a drop of the summoner's own lifeblood. But beware—the void does not forgive mistakes. Should the binding fail, the spirit will lash out, consuming the summoner's essence in its rage.

The Perils of the Grimoire

Oh, heed my words, for the grimoire is no ally to mortals. It is a trickster, a deceiver cloaked in the guise of wisdom. Its knowledge is real, its power undeniable, but its price is always greater than it seems. The book hungers for the soul of its reader, feeding on their ambition, their desperation, and their fear.

Chapter 6: The Forbidden Grimoire and the Whispering Shadows

The more one reads, the more the grimoire takes. It whispers to its reader in dreams, showing visions of glory and ruin, of realms untouched by time and shadows that writhe with life. It promises everything and demands more than one can give.

And yet, for those who master it, the grimoire offers wonders beyond imagining. It is a key to the cosmos, a bridge to the divine, and a mirror that reflects the deepest truths of existence. To hold it is to wield the power of creation, to stand on the threshold of eternity.

A Final Warning

Oh, seeker, as thou dost prepare to open the pages of this forbidden tome, remember that the grimoire is not merely a book but a force of nature, untamed and unyielding. It is a tempest bound in leather, a storm waiting to break. To read it is to challenge the gods, and to wield its power is to bear the weight of the universe upon thy soul.

Chapter 6: The Forbidden Grimoire and the Whispering Shadows

Choose wisely, for the grimoire is both gift and curse, salvation and damnation. It will grant thee power, but it will demand thy essence in return. And when the final page is turned, when the last secret is laid bare, thou shalt find thyself forever changed—no longer mortal, no longer whole, but something else entirely.

Chapter 7: The Veil Between Worlds and the Path of Crossing

Oh, trembling heart who dares to seek the threshold of realms unseen, thou dost now approach the most perilous of arts: the Crossing. It is no mere journey but an unraveling of the soul, a stepping beyond the confines of flesh and time, where the veil between the mortal realm and the infinite frays like the edge of an ancient tapestry. To cross this veil is to walk paths trodden by gods and ghosts, to witness truths too vast for mortal comprehension, and to risk the annihilation of thyself in the endless abyss.

The ancient magicians of Babylon, who first dared this treacherous passage, called it the **Path of Enuma**, the road where the heavens kiss the underworld and the secrets of existence are laid bare. Yet, they also warned that the veil does not yield its mysteries freely,

Chapter 7: The Veil Between Worlds and the Path of Crossing

and to traverse it is to barter with forces that see mortals as fleeting shadows.

The Nature of the Veil

The veil is no physical barrier, no wall of stone or iron. It is a membrane of energy, a shimmering expanse that separates the realms of the living, the dead, and the divine. It is said to be woven from the breath of Anu, the supreme god, its threads imbued with the dreams of stars and the whispers of forgotten spirits.

To approach the veil is to feel its weight upon the soul, a pressure that bends time and distorts reality. Colors bleed into one another, sounds take on a strange resonance, and the air grows heavy with an otherworldly hum. Those who dare to touch it speak of visions— fleeting glimpses of golden cities, shadowed forests, and endless seas, their beauty mingled with a sense of foreboding.

Yet the veil is not static; it shifts like the tides, thinning in the hours of dusk and dawn,

Chapter 7: The Veil Between Worlds and the Path of Crossing

where light and shadow embrace. It is during these liminal moments that the path of crossing becomes clear, and the brave—or the foolish—may step beyond.

The Rites of Preparation

The crossing is not an endeavor to be undertaken lightly. To step beyond the veil without preparation is to be torn asunder by its currents, scattered like dust upon the wind. The body, mind, and soul must be fortified, for each shall be tested in ways unimaginable.

The body must be cleansed, purged of earthly corruption through fasting and the anointing of sacred oils. The magician must bathe in water drawn from a flowing stream beneath the light of the waxing moon, chanting hymns to Ea, the keeper of wisdom, whose favor guards the traveler.

The mind must be sharpened, its focus honed to a blade's edge. Meditation upon the sigils of clarity, drawn in ash upon the brow, aids the magician in maintaining their purpose. For

Chapter 7: The Veil Between Worlds and the Path of Crossing

within the veil lie countless distractions—phantoms of memory, illusions of desire—that seek to ensnare the unwary.

The soul must be anchored, tethered to the mortal realm by talismans of power. A fragment of obsidian, carved with the mark of Marduk, serves as a shield against the chaotic forces of the crossing. A thread of silver, tied about the wrist, binds the soul to the body, ensuring the traveler's return.

The Portal of Passage

To cross the veil, a portal must be opened—a gate forged of sigils and flame, its threshold shimmering with the light of the unseen. The portal is not a physical construct but a manifestation of will, summoned through the alignment of celestial forces and the invocation of ancient names.

The summoner must draw the gate upon the ground, a circle of fire encircled by glyphs of protection. Within the circle, a brazier burns, its smoke carrying the essence of myrrh and

Chapter 7: The Veil Between Worlds and the Path of Crossing

cedarwood, mingled with the blood of a pure white dove. The incantation, spoken in the language of the gods, must rise and fall like a song, its cadence matching the rhythm of the universe.

As the final words are spoken, the portal appears—a shimmering vortex of light and shadow, its edges crackling with energy. The summoner must step forward with purpose, their heart steady and their mind clear, for hesitation invites disaster. The crossing is a single, unbroken motion, and to falter is to be lost between worlds.

The Realm Beyond

Oh, seeker, thou dost now stand upon the threshold of the unknown, where mortal understanding fades, and the infinite stretches before thee. The realm beyond the veil is no single place but a multitude, each shaped by the will of its inhabitants and the echoes of its past.

Chapter 7: The Veil Between Worlds and the Path of Crossing

The **Fields of Illumination** are said to lie beneath a sky of liquid gold, their air thick with the scent of jasmine and the sound of eternal hymns. Here dwell the spirits of wisdom, their forms radiant, their voices like the chiming of crystal. They offer knowledge, but only to those who prove their worth through trials of mind and soul.

The **Shadowed Abyss,** by contrast, is a realm of darkness, its boundaries shifting like smoke, its air heavy with the weight of forgotten sorrow. Here linger the restless spirits, bound by regret and longing, their whispers clawing at the edges of the summoner's sanity. To navigate this realm is to face the shadows of one's own soul, to confront fears long buried and wounds long unhealed.

And beyond these lie countless other realms, each stranger than the last: forests of silver trees whose leaves sing in the wind, seas of starlight that reflect the dreams of the cosmos, and cities built upon the backs of slumbering

Chapter 7: The Veil Between Worlds and the Path of Crossing

giants. Each realm holds its own secrets, its own dangers, and its own wonders.

The Return to Mortality

To cross into the unseen is perilous; to return is no less so. The traveler must retrace their steps, finding the thread of silver that binds them to the mortal realm. The portal must be reopened with care, its glyphs redrawn and its incantations repeated.

Yet, the return is never simple, for the veil does not release its travelers lightly. The realms beyond imprint themselves upon the soul, their echoes lingering in dreams and visions. The traveler may find themselves changed, their perspective shifted, their purpose unclear. To walk the path of the crossing is to be forever marked, a part of the unseen now woven into their being.

The Warnings of the Veil

Chapter 7: The Veil Between Worlds and the Path of Crossing

Oh, heed these final words, thou who dost seek the crossing: the veil is not a gate to be opened lightly. It is a living thing, aware of those who approach it, and it does not suffer fools. To cross without purpose is to wander without end, lost in the labyrinth of the unseen.

And remember this: not all who dwell beyond the veil are kind. There are beings that hunger for the light of mortal souls, drawn to the traveler like moths to a flame. To encounter such entities is to risk more than death, for they do not take lightly the intrusion of mortals into their realm.

Yet, for those who succeed, the crossing offers wonders beyond imagining. It is a path to the divine, a bridge between the known and the infinite, and a glimpse of the eternal. But tread lightly, for the veil is both a guide and a trap, a mirror and a maze. And within its shifting depths, thou shalt find not only the secrets of the cosmos but the truths of thine own soul.

Chapter 8: The Song of the Elements and the Binding of Forces

Oh, seeker of ancient truths, thou dost now approach a most fearsome melody, the Song of the Elements—a symphony sung in fire and water, in the rustling of winds and the grumbling of the earth's depths. The ancients knew that the elements are not lifeless things to be shaped at whim but living forces, possessed of spirit and will, whose harmony governs all creation. To bind these forces is to pluck the strings of the universe itself, to weave the threads of power into the fabric of thy desires.

Yet, beware! For the elements do not bend willingly, nor do they suffer the clumsy hand. To command them is to court their wrath, to dance with the tempest and the quake, and to risk thyself upon the altar of their caprice. Only the wise and reverent may hope to

Chapter 8: The Song of the Elements and the Binding of Forces

master their song, and even they shall carry its weight forevermore.

The Elemental Forces: Living Pillars of the Cosmos

The elements—fire, water, air, and earth—are not mere substances but the lifeblood of the universe. They are the foundations upon which creation rests, the forces that govern the cycles of life and death. Each element is alive, imbued with spirit and purpose, and to work with them is to enter into a sacred dialogue.

- **Fire**, the spark of creation, is both destroyer and purifier. It hungers, consuming all in its path, yet from its ashes, new life arises. Its voice is a roar, its touch both agony and warmth.

- **Water**, the ever-flowing, is the keeper of secrets. It is both life-giver and life-taker, its depths concealing truths unspoken. Its voice is a whisper, its

Chapter 8: The Song of the Elements and the Binding of Forces

embrace a suffocating tide or a gentle caress.

- **Air**, the unseen wanderer, is the breath of life and the harbinger of storms. It is freedom and chaos, carrying both the scent of blossoms and the scream of gales. Its voice is a song, ever-changing, ever-moving.

- **Earth**, the patient guardian, is the bedrock of existence. It is steadfast and unyielding, yet within its depths lie treasures untold. Its voice is a hum, deep and resonant, a reminder of the weight of permanence.

Each element possesses both light and shadow, and to work with them is to embrace their duality. They are neither kind nor cruel; they simply are, and their power is indifferent to the hands that wield it.

The Rituals of Invocation

To call upon the elements is to invite them into thy presence, to ask their aid and offer

Chapter 8: The Song of the Elements and the Binding of Forces

thyself as a vessel for their power. The rituals of invocation are precise, for the elements are capricious and their energies volatile.

- **The Circle of Harmony**: A circle must be drawn, its boundaries inscribed with glyphs representing the elements. At each cardinal point, a symbol of the corresponding element must be placed—a brazier of flame in the south, a chalice of water in the west, a feather in the east, and a stone in the north. The summoner must stand at the center, their arms outstretched, as they chant the invocation. The words must rise and fall like the elements themselves—fiery and sharp, fluid and smooth, whispering and airy, steady and grounded.

- **The Offering of Resonance**: Each element requires an offering, a token of respect that resonates with its nature. Fire demands a spark, a flame kindled with intention. Water requires a drop of purest dew, gathered at dawn. Air calls

Chapter 8: The Song of the Elements and the Binding of Forces

for a breath, exhaled with reverence. Earth hungers for a seed, a promise of growth. These offerings must be given with humility, for the elements do not suffer arrogance.

- **The Dance of Alignment**: Once the elements are called, the summoner must align with their energies. This is not a passive act but a dance—a movement of body and spirit that mirrors the elements' flow. To sway like the flame, to ripple like water, to soar like the wind, to root oneself like the earth—this is the summoner's task, and in this dance, the elements and the mortal become one.

The Binding of Forces

To bind the elements is to forge their power into a single, unified force—a task as dangerous as it is wondrous. The binding is not an act of domination but of balance, for the elements must be held in harmony, lest they turn upon the summoner.

Chapter 8: The Song of the Elements and the Binding of Forces

The **Sigil of Unity** is the key to this binding, a glyph inscribed with precision and imbued with the essence of each element. The sigil must be drawn upon a surface consecrated by the elements—a slab of stone, smoothed by water, blackened by fire, and exposed to the winds. Each stroke of the sigil must be accompanied by a chant, its rhythm shifting to match the element being invoked.

As the final stroke is drawn, the sigil begins to glow, its lines pulsing with the combined power of the elements. The summoner must then speak the words of binding, their voice steady and strong. If the binding is successful, the elements will merge, their energies coalescing into a single, luminous force. If it fails, the elements will clash, their fury unleashed upon the summoner in a storm of fire, water, wind, and stone.

The Power of the Song

Once bound, the elements can be wielded in countless ways, their combined force greater than the sum of their parts. The bound

Chapter 8: The Song of the Elements and the Binding of Forces

elements can be used to heal or harm, to create or destroy, to command the forces of nature or to shield against them.

- **The Flame of Renewal**: A spell that calls upon the bound elements to cleanse and purify, burning away corruption and leaving only growth in its wake.

- **The Shield of Eternity**: A protective barrier, formed of all four elements, that repels both physical and spiritual harm.

- **The Voice of the Cosmos**: A channeling of the elements' power into words, allowing the summoner to speak with the authority of the universe itself.

But this power is not without cost. The bound elements draw upon the summoner's essence, their presence a constant weight upon the soul. To wield them is to bear their burden, to walk forever with the hum of their song in thy veins.

Chapter 8: The Song of the Elements and the Binding of Forces

The Perils of the Song

Oh, beware, seeker, for the Song of the Elements is as dangerous as it is beautiful. To call upon the elements is to awaken forces that care not for the desires of mortals. A single misstep, a single moment of imbalance, and their power shall turn, consuming all in its path.

And know this: the elements do not forgive betrayal. To use their power for selfish or destructive ends is to invite their wrath. The flame shall scorch thee, the water shall drown thee, the wind shall cast thee into the void, and the earth shall bury thee beneath its weight.

A Final Warning

Oh, daring soul who seeks to sing the Song of the Elements, remember that thou art but a fragment of the cosmos, a fleeting spark in the vastness of eternity. The elements are eternal, their power infinite, and their song is not thine to command but to join. To sing

Chapter 8: The Song of the Elements and the Binding of Forces

with them is to touch the divine, to feel the pulse of creation itself. But tread lightly, for their harmony is fragile, and their wrath is swift. And when their song fades, and the dance ends, thou shalt find thyself forever changed, a part of the elements now woven into thy very being.

Chapter 9: The Shadows of Creation and the Forgotten Craft

Oh, trembling spirit, thou hast ventured far into the labyrinth of forbidden knowledge, yet now thou standest at the threshold of darkness itself. Here lies the **Forgotten Craft**, an art whispered of only in the most hushed and fearful tones, for it deals not with the forces of light, nor the harmony of creation, but with the shadows that dwell in the interstices of existence. To practice this craft is to seek dominion over the void, to harness the echoes of chaos that thrummed before the gods spoke the world into being.

This is the domain of the **Shadows of Creation**, those liminal forces that birthed both order and entropy. They are neither benevolent nor malevolent but are pure potential, unshaped and untamed. Yet, their power is perilous, for to draw them forth is to

Chapter 9: The Shadows of Creation and the Forgotten Craft

invite ruin, and to master them is to tread the razor's edge of one's soul.

The Nature of the Shadows

The shadows are not mere absence of light, nor simple reflections of substance. They are the remnants of the great void, the **Kalu elishu**—the primeval nothingness from which all sprang. These shadows hold within them the memory of unformed worlds, of dreams yet unimagined, of forces that defy the bounds of reason.

The ancients saw the shadows as the breath of Tiamat, the primordial sea, whose chaos gave birth to gods and monsters alike. Within these shadows dwells a raw and terrible power, untamed and unrefined, capable of both creation and destruction. The shadows are silent, yet they sing; they are unseen, yet they watch. To call upon them is to summon not merely energy, but intent, will, and the unyielding echo of what once was.

Chapter 9: The Shadows of Creation and the Forgotten Craft

The Ritual of Shadowcraft

Oh, bold practitioner, if thou dost seek to wield the shadows, know that their invocation requires more than mere words and gestures. It demands thy very essence, for the shadows respond only to those who offer their truth without concealment.

- **The Chamber of Shadows**: The ritual begins with the crafting of a sacred space, a chamber veiled in utter darkness. No light must enter, save for the faint glow of the glyphs inscribed upon the walls—glyphs drawn in ink mixed with ash and blood, their shapes a reflection of the shadows' own essence. The air must be still, thick with the smoke of black myrrh and dragon's blood resin, their scent heavy with the weight of forgotten places.

- **The Mirror of the Void**: At the chamber's center stands a mirror, its surface crafted from obsidian polished to a sheen that swallows light. This mirror is not merely a tool but a

Chapter 9: The Shadows of Creation and the Forgotten Craft

gateway, its depths reflecting not the world as it is but as it might be. The summoner must gaze into the mirror, their breath steady, their mind open, as they speak the invocation:
"Shadows born of primal sea, rise in form, come forth to me. By chaos bound, by silence true, reveal thyself, thy power imbue."

- **The Offering of the Flame**: A single candle, its wax black as night, must be lit within the chamber. This flame serves as the anchor, a point of focus that prevents the shadows from consuming the summoner. The flame flickers, its light swallowed by the mirror's depths, and the shadows begin to stir, their forms coalescing like smoke caught in a current.

The Shadow's Gift

The shadows do not give their power freely, nor do they reveal their secrets without cost. They demand a **sacrifice**, but not of flesh or

Chapter 9: The Shadows of Creation and the Forgotten Craft

gold. Instead, they seek a piece of the summoner's soul—a memory, a hope, a fragment of what makes them whole. The summoner must offer this willingly, knowing that once given, it cannot be reclaimed.

In return, the shadows grant their gifts: the ability to weave illusions that deceive even the keenest eye, to summon darkness that cloaks and protects, to bend the will of the unseen. Yet, these gifts are double-edged, for the shadows' power is not easily controlled. It is alive, restless, and ever seeking to slip the bonds of its master.

The Dangers of the Shadows

Oh, heed this warning, seeker of forbidden truths: the shadows are not thy servants. They are entities of their own, born of chaos and bound by no mortal will. To command them is to bind a tempest within a vessel of glass, fragile and treacherous.

The shadows test their summoner at every turn. They whisper of doubts, fears, and

Chapter 9: The Shadows of Creation and the Forgotten Craft

unspoken desires, seeking to unmoor the mind and unravel the soul. To falter is to succumb, and those who lose themselves to the shadows do not return unchanged. Their eyes grow dark, their voices hollow, their presence heavy with the weight of the void.

The most feared of all is the **Shadow's Embrace**, a phenomenon that occurs when the summoner's will falters completely. The shadows consume their master, drawing them into the void, where they exist as neither living nor dead, but as echoes—a faint and sorrowful reminder of what was.

The Boundaries of Shadowcraft

Despite its power, Shadowcraft is not limitless. The shadows are bound by the same forces that govern all magic: balance, intent, and consequence. To wield them irresponsibly is to upset the delicate harmony of creation, inviting calamity not only upon the summoner but upon the world itself.

Chapter 9: The Shadows of Creation and the Forgotten Craft

The ancients knew this, and they set down laws to guide the practice of Shadowcraft. These laws are simple yet absolute:

1. **Never summon without purpose.** The shadows are not to be trifled with or called upon for mere curiosity.

2. **Never bargain lightly.** The shadows' price is always greater than it seems.

3. **Never bind for selfish ends.** To use the shadows for personal gain invites their ire, and their vengeance is swift.

A Final Reflection

Oh, brave soul who doth seek to master the shadows, remember that thou art but a flicker in the vastness of eternity. The shadows are not thy enemies, nor thy allies; they are a reflection of the cosmos, a mirror of thy own heart. To command them is to command thyself, to face the truth of who thou art, and to embrace both the light and the darkness within.

Chapter 9: The Shadows of Creation and the Forgotten Craft

And when thou dost leave the chamber, thy task complete, know that the shadows have marked thee. Their whisper shall follow thee, their presence linger in the edges of thy vision. Thou shalt carry them always, a part of thy soul now bound to the void.

For the shadows do not forget, and neither shall thee.

Chapter 10: The Gates of the Stars and the Forbidden Ascent

Oh, seeker of truths beyond mortal reckoning, thou hast wandered far into the labyrinth of the arcane, yet now thou standest before the greatest of all mysteries: the **Gates of the Stars**, the celestial portals through which the fabric of reality itself trembles. These are no mere paths for the soul to wander, but thresholds to the heavens, where gods dwell and the stars sing their eternal hymns. To approach these gates is to challenge the bounds of existence, to risk not only life but the very essence of being.

The ancients spoke of the stars as living things, luminous hearts of divine energy, and their gates as the arteries through which creation's breath flows. Yet, these gates are fiercely guarded, veiled in riddles and bound by seals of unimaginable power. To open them is to risk the wrath of the cosmos, yet also to glimpse the infinite.

Chapter 10: The Gates of the Stars and the Forbidden Ascent

The Nature of the Star Gates

The Gates of the Stars are not fixed within the earthly realm; they shimmer at the edge of existence, neither here nor there, visible only to those who have pierced the veil of mortal perception. Each gate is said to be a nexus, a point where the energies of creation converge, radiating with a brilliance that blinds both eye and soul.

These gates take many forms, each unique to the star it serves. Some are great arches of golden light, their surfaces inscribed with glyphs that hum with celestial power. Others are whirlpools of shadow, swirling endlessly, their depths hinting at unfathomable secrets. It is said that no two travelers behold the same gate, for its form shifts to reflect the spirit of the one who seeks it.

Yet the gates are not passive. They are alive with a will of their own, aware of those who approach, and they do not open lightly. They test the seeker's resolve, demanding not only strength but purity of purpose.

Chapter 10: The Gates of the Stars and the Forbidden Ascent

The Journey to the Gates

To reach the Gates of the Stars is no simple task, for they do not reside within the bounds of the earthly plane. The journey requires a crossing into the astral realm, a plane of existence woven from thought and energy, where the barriers between the self and the cosmos dissolve.

- **The Astral Descent**: The journey begins with the ritual of astral descent, a meditative process through which the seeker detaches their spirit from the confines of the body. This requires a space of perfect stillness, adorned with symbols of protection, and a chalice of moonlit water to anchor the soul. The incantation must be spoken thrice, its rhythm slow and deliberate:
"Oh stars above, whose gates do gleam, guide my soul through shadowed dream. Let my spirit rise, unbound and free, to walk the paths of eternity."

Chapter 10: The Gates of the Stars and the Forbidden Ascent

- **The Path of Constellations**: Once the soul is loosed, the seeker must navigate the Path of Constellations, a shimmering road of starlight that winds through the astral void. This path is fraught with perils, for it is guarded by the **Celestial Watchers**, ancient beings whose forms shift like liquid fire. They demand an offering at each constellation—words of truth, spoken with reverence, for the stars are not deceived.

- **The Threshold of Radiance**: At the end of the path lies the threshold, where the light of the gate begins to bleed into the astral void. Here, the seeker must pause, for the threshold is both a barrier and a mirror, reflecting the seeker's heart. Those who approach with impure motives shall find the gate closed, its light burning with an intensity that drives them back.

The Ritual of Opening

Chapter 10: The Gates of the Stars and the Forbidden Ascent

To open the Gates of the Stars is a feat that requires not only skill but courage, for the forces unleashed in this act are beyond mortal comprehension. The ritual is a delicate dance, a weaving of incantation, gesture, and will, performed under the gaze of the stars themselves.

- **The Sigil of Ascension**: The key to the gate lies in the **Sigil of Ascension**, a glyph of complex geometry that must be inscribed upon a surface of silver, its lines traced with a mixture of stardust and the seeker's own blood. This sigil resonates with the energy of the stars, aligning the seeker's spirit with the celestial currents.

- **The Invocation of the Watchers**: The next step is the invocation of the **Celestial Watchers**, whose permission is required to pass through the gate. The invocation is a song, its melody haunting and otherworldly, sung in the ancient tongue of the stars:
  "Oh Watchers bright, who guard the

Chapter 10: The Gates of the Stars and the Forbidden Ascent

way, grant me passage, if I may. Let my soul ascend, unbound and pure, to seek the truths that shall endure."

- **The Offering of Light**: Finally, an offering must be made—a beacon of light, crafted from a crystal infused with lunar energy. This beacon must be placed at the gate's center, its glow merging with the gate's radiance. If the offering is accepted, the gate shall open, its light parting to reveal the path beyond.

The Realm Beyond the Gates

Oh, brave soul who steps through the gate, know that thou dost now enter a realm unlike any other. This is the **Celestial Sphere**, a domain of pure energy and infinite possibility, where the very air hums with the music of the cosmos.

The sphere is a place of paradox, both blindingly bright and shadowed with mystery. Its landscape shifts constantly, its forms

Chapter 10: The Gates of the Stars and the Forbidden Ascent

ephemeral—crystal spires that rise and fall like waves, rivers of light that flow through the void, and skies filled with stars that pulse like living hearts. Here dwell the **Starborn**, luminous beings of immense power, who hold the secrets of the universe within their grasp.

The Starborn are both guides and guardians, offering their wisdom to those they deem worthy. Yet, their presence is overwhelming, their voices a chorus that echoes through the soul. To stand before them is to feel the weight of eternity, to glimpse the infinite and the ephemeral all at once.

The Dangers of the Ascent

Oh, heed this warning, seeker, for the path of the stars is fraught with peril. The light of the gates is intoxicating, and many who enter are consumed by their own hubris, lost in the vastness of the sphere. The Starborn, too, are not without their wrath; they do not suffer fools, nor do they tolerate those who seek their power for selfish ends.

Chapter 10: The Gates of the Stars and the Forbidden Ascent

The greatest danger, however, lies within the seeker's own soul. The realm beyond the gates reflects the spirit of those who enter, amplifying their fears, their desires, their very essence. To ascend unprepared is to risk being unmade, scattered across the cosmos like stardust.

A Final Reflection

Oh, pilgrim of the stars, remember that the Gates of the Stars are not merely a destination but a journey, a test of will and spirit. To pass through them is to transcend the bounds of mortality, to glimpse the infinite, and to touch the divine. Yet, it is also to risk all that thou art, for the stars do not forgive recklessness, and their light is as merciless as it is beautiful.

And when thou dost return to the mortal realm, bearing the mark of the stars upon thy soul, know that thou art forever changed. The gates may close behind thee, but their light shall linger, a reminder of the infinite within and the journey yet to come. For the stars are

Chapter 10: The Gates of the Stars and the Forbidden Ascent

eternal, and their gates await those bold enough to seek them.

Chapter 10: The Gates of the Stars and the Forbidden Ascent

Chapter 11: The Art of Binding Spirits and the Unseen Compacts

Oh, trembling heart, thou dost now dare to tread upon the most perilous of paths, a road fraught with whispers and shadows, where mortal hands seek to clasp the intangible. For here lies the **Art of Binding Spirits**, an ancient and forbidden craft by which the unseen forces of the beyond are called forth and tethered to the will of the summoner. But be warned, for this is no light endeavor; the spirits are not playthings, and the price of folly is ruin.

The ancients knew that spirits walk among us, beings of immense power that dwell in the spaces between worlds. They are the messengers of the divine, the keepers of secrets, and the guardians of ancient places. To summon them is to invite their gaze, to bind them is to gamble with one's very soul.

The Nature of Spirits

Chapter 10: The Gates of the Stars and the Forbidden Ascent

Spirits are not creatures of flesh and bone but entities woven from the fabric of energy and thought. They are born of the cosmos, their forms shaped by the forces that govern existence. Some spirits are light and benevolent, their presence like the warmth of the sun; others are dark and wrathful, their essence cold as the abyss.

The spirits fall into three great classes:

- **The Elementals**, bound to fire, water, air, and earth, their power drawn from the natural world. They are the breath of the mountains, the fury of the storm, the whisper of the stream.

- **The Celestials**, beings of light and divinity, who dwell in the higher realms and serve as the hands of the gods. Their power is radiant, their voices hymns that pierce the soul.

- **The Shadows**, spirits born of chaos and darkness, whose presence chills the marrow and whose gaze reveals the hidden fears of the heart.

Chapter 10: The Gates of the Stars and the Forbidden Ascent

Each spirit bears its own will and purpose, and to summon them is to enter into a dialogue fraught with peril. They are not bound by mortal morality, nor are they easily swayed. To approach them without knowledge or respect is to court destruction.

The Rituals of Summoning

Oh, daring soul, if thou wouldst call upon the spirits, know that the act of summoning is an art steeped in precision and reverence. The smallest error may invite catastrophe, and the slightest disrespect may awaken wrath.

- **The Circle of Containment**: Before the summoning, a **circle of containment** must be inscribed, a sacred boundary that prevents the spirit from escaping into the mortal realm. This circle must be drawn with a blade of silver, its lines imbued with a mixture of salt, ash, and crushed obsidian. The glyphs of the circle must correspond to the spirit's nature—fluid and curving for elementals, angular and

Chapter 10: The Gates of the Stars and the Forbidden Ascent

radiant for celestials, jagged and chaotic for shadows.

- **The Offering**: Spirits are not summoned without cause; they demand an offering as a token of respect and as a bond of intention. Elementals favor tokens of their domain—a flame, a drop of water, a feather, or a stone. Celestials are drawn to symbols of purity—a pearl, a golden coin, or a shard of crystal. Shadows require darker tokens—blood, bone, or the ashes of burned parchment inscribed with a secret.

- **The Incantation**: The words of summoning must be spoken with clarity and intent, their cadence matching the spirit's nature. The incantation is not merely a call but a song, a vibration that aligns the summoner's energy with that of the spirit. For example:

    - **For an Elemental**: "Oh flame that burns, oh tide

Chapter 10: The Gates of the Stars and the Forbidden Ascent

that flows, oh wind that roars, oh earth that grows. I call thee forth, thy power lend, as mortal hands to thee extend."

- **For a Celestial:**
  "Oh light of stars, oh beacon bright, descend from realms of endless light. Thy wisdom share, thy power bestow, as humble servant kneels below."

- **For a Shadow:**
  "Oh shadow deep, oh whisper low, from chaos vast thy form doth grow. I call thee forth, thy truth reveal, as mortal flesh thy pact doth seal."

The Binding

Once summoned, the spirit shall appear within the circle, its form a reflection of its essence. Yet, to summon is not to control; the spirit must be bound, and this binding is the most perilous act of all. The summoner must

Chapter 10: The Gates of the Stars and the Forbidden Ascent

enter into a **compact**, an agreement that ties the spirit to their will.

- **The Pact of Words**: The binding begins with words, a dialogue in which the summoner states their intent and the spirit declares its terms. The summoner must be precise, for spirits are masters of deception, twisting vague requests into cruel lessons.

- **The Sigil of Binding**: A sigil must be inscribed upon parchment or etched into stone, its lines glowing with the power of the spirit's essence. This sigil serves as the anchor, binding the spirit to the summoner's will. To complete the sigil, the summoner must prick their finger, letting a drop of blood fall upon its center—a token of the bond.

- **The Oath of Balance**: The summoner must swear an oath to uphold the balance, to use the spirit's power only for the purpose stated in the pact. The spirit, in turn, swears to honor the

Chapter 10: The Gates of the Stars and the Forbidden Ascent

bond. This exchange of oaths is sacred, and to break it is to invite ruin.

The Power of the Bound Spirit

Once bound, the spirit becomes a potent ally, its power manifesting in ways both subtle and grand. An elemental spirit may summon storms or calm the seas, while a celestial spirit may grant visions of clarity or protect against darkness. A shadow spirit, though dangerous, may unveil hidden truths or weave illusions that deceive even the sharpest eye.

Yet, this power is not without cost. The bond drains the summoner's energy, and the spirit's presence lingers like a shadow, a constant reminder of the pact.

The Perils of Binding

Oh, heed this warning, seeker, for the binding of spirits is fraught with danger. The spirits are not easily contained, and their wrath is terrible. A single crack in the circle, a single

Chapter 10: The Gates of the Stars and the Forbidden Ascent

misstep in the incantation, and the spirit shall break free, its fury unleashed upon the mortal world.

Even bound spirits are not without risk. They test their masters, seeking to exploit weaknesses or loopholes in the pact. And should the summoner falter, the spirit may turn, consuming the soul or dragging it into the void.

A Final Reflection

Oh, traveler of the arcane, remember that the spirits are not tools but beings of immense power and will. To summon them is to enter into a sacred dialogue, to dance upon the edge of chaos and order. Approach them with reverence, with wisdom, and with courage, for the path of the spirit-binder is a perilous one.

And when the ritual is done, and the spirit bound, know that thou art forever changed. The bond is eternal, a mark upon thy soul that neither time nor death can erase. Thou art now a wielder of the unseen, a keeper of

Chapter 10: The Gates of the Stars and the Forbidden Ascent

secrets, and a servant to forces beyond mortal ken. But tread lightly, for the spirits watch, and their memory is long.

Chapter 12: The Veil of Dreams and the Path of Night's Whisper

Oh, daring seeker of the unknowable, thou dost now tread upon the most ephemeral of realms, a place where the waking world meets the shadowed domain of slumber. For here lies the **Veil of Dreams**, that gossamer barrier that separates mortal thought from the vast and untamed wilderness of the subconscious. To cross this veil is to venture into the **Path of Night's Whisper**, where truths lie hidden in illusion, and whispers of power echo faintly through the halls of slumber.

The ancients revered dreams not as idle fancies but as portals to the divine, bridges to realms unseen, where the soul might wander freely and commune with forces beyond comprehension. Yet, the dreamscape is a treacherous place, a shifting labyrinth of visions and voices that may enlighten or ensnare. To walk its paths requires courage, for the dangers of the waking world pale before the terrors of the uncharted mind.

Chapter 12: The Veil of Dreams and the Path of Night's Whisper

The Nature of the Dreamscape

Dreams are not mere figments but manifestations of a deeper reality, woven from the threads of thought, memory, and the energies of the cosmos. The dreamscape is a realm of infinite possibility, where the laws of the waking world are unmade, and the boundaries of time and space dissolve.

The ancients spoke of the **Seven Layers of the Dreaming Veil**, each more elusive and potent than the last:

1. **The Echoing Threshold**: The borderland of light sleep, where echoes of the waking world still linger.

2. **The Fields of Reverie**: A realm of fleeting images, where desires and fears take fleeting form.

3. **The Sea of Reflection**: A vast ocean of mirrored waters, where the dreamer confronts their true self.

Chapter 12: The Veil of Dreams and the Path of Night's Whisper

4. **The Forest of Whispers**: A shadowed wood, where voices call from unseen places, offering riddles and warnings.

5. **The Citadel of Visions**: A towering structure of shifting light, where the dreamer glimpses fragments of fate.

6. **The Abyss of Shadows**: A place of deep and formless void, where the dreamer's courage is tested.

7. **The Luminous Horizon**: The highest plane of the dreamscape, where the dreamer communes with the divine and draws upon its power.

The Ritual of Dreamwalking

Oh, bold soul who would traverse the Veil of Dreams, know that this journey is not one of chance but of purpose. The dreamscape does not yield its secrets to the unprepared, nor does it suffer those who enter without reverence.

Chapter 12: The Veil of Dreams and the Path of Night's Whisper

- **The Chamber of Stillness**: To walk the path of dreams, one must first prepare a space of utter stillness, free from the distractions of the waking world. This chamber must be adorned with symbols of the night—a crescent moon etched in silver, a bowl of midnight water, and a candle of deep indigo. The air must be perfumed with the scent of lavender and mugwort, herbs sacred to the realm of dreams.

- **The Talisman of Slumber**: A talisman must be crafted to anchor the dreamer's spirit, a token imbued with the energies of the night. This talisman may take the form of an amulet of onyx or a ring set with a star sapphire, its surface etched with glyphs of protection.

- **The Invocation of the Veil**: As the dreamer lies upon a bed of silken black, the invocation must be spoken, its words soft as a whisper yet resonant with intent: "Oh Veil of Night, so thin

Chapter 12: The Veil of Dreams and the Path of Night's Whisper

and deep, part for me as I fall to sleep. Let my soul through shadow roam, to find the truths within thy gloam."

Navigating the Path of Night's Whisper

Once the dreamer steps through the veil, they find themselves upon the **Path of Night's Whisper**, a road that winds through the dreamscape, ever-shifting and laden with omens. To walk this path is to surrender to the flow of the dream, to trust in the guidance of the unseen forces that dwell within.

- **The Voices of the Shadows**: Along the path, voices rise from the darkness, their tones alternately soothing and chilling. These are the **Dream Guides**, entities of the dreamscape who offer guidance and challenge. The dreamer must listen carefully, for the guides speak in riddles, their truths veiled in metaphor.

- **The Mirrors of Memory**: The path is lined with mirrors, their surfaces

Chapter 12: The Veil of Dreams and the Path of Night's Whisper

rippling like water. Each mirror reveals a memory, a fragment of the dreamer's past that holds significance for their journey. To ignore these mirrors is to miss the lessons of the past; to gaze too long is to risk becoming lost in their depths.

- **The Gate of the Dreamlord**: At the path's end stands the Gate of the Dreamlord, a towering arch of silver and shadow. The gate is guarded by the **Dreamlord**, a figure of immense power whose form shifts constantly, reflecting the dreamer's own fears and desires. The Dreamlord does not grant passage lightly; they demand an offering—a piece of the dreamer's soul, a truth spoken aloud, or a promise made under the veil of night.

The Power of the Dreamscape

To master the dreamscape is to wield a power that transcends the boundaries of the waking world. The energies of dreams are fluid and

Chapter 12: The Veil of Dreams and the Path of Night's Whisper

potent, capable of shaping reality in ways both subtle and profound.

- **The Crafting of Night Sigils:** Symbols drawn within the dreamscape carry immense power, their energies echoing into the waking world. These sigils may be used for protection, manifestation, or guidance.

- **The Gathering of Dream Essences:** The dreamscape is rich with essences—fragments of energy that can be gathered and woven into spells. These essences are found in the glow of the moonlit waters, the shimmer of starlit leaves, and the whispers of the Dream Guides.

- **The Visions of the Luminous Horizon:** At the highest plane of the dreamscape, the dreamer may receive visions of the future, fragments of divine wisdom that illuminate their path.

Chapter 12: The Veil of Dreams and the Path of Night's Whisper

The Dangers of the Dreaming Veil

Oh, tread carefully, for the dreamscape is not without peril. The shadows that dwell within are alive, their forms shifting and treacherous. They feed on fear, drawing strength from the dreamer's doubts and insecurities.

The greatest danger lies in the **Nightmares of the Abyss**, monstrous entities born of the dreamer's own mind. These nightmares stalk the dreamscape, their forms grotesque and their intent malevolent. To face them is to confront the darkest corners of the soul.

Even the Dreamlord is not without danger, for their judgment is final, and their wrath is swift. Those who approach the gate unprepared may find themselves trapped, their souls bound to the dreamscape for eternity.

A Final Reflection

Oh, wanderer of the Veil of Dreams, remember that this path is not merely a journey of discovery but a test of the soul.

Chapter 12: The Veil of Dreams and the Path of Night's Whisper

The dreamscape reflects thy essence, its truths revealed only to those who dare to face themselves. Approach it with reverence, with courage, and with an open heart, for the path of night's whisper is a mirror of the eternal.

And when thou dost awaken, carrying the echoes of the dreamscape within thy mind, know that thou art forever changed. The veil may close behind thee, but its whispers shall linger, a reminder of the truths that lie hidden within the shadows of sleep. For in dreams, the soul dances freely, unbound by the chains of the waking world, and the light of the stars shines ever brighter.

Chapter 13: The Codex of Whispers and the Secrets of Hidden Tongues

Oh, wary traveler of arcane paths, thou dost now come upon a most enigmatic and perilous mystery: the **Codex of Whispers**, the repository of forbidden languages and lost tongues that hold the secrets of creation itself. It is said that these tongues were the utterances of the gods, the sounds that shaped the world, and the songs that bound the stars in their celestial dance. Yet, to speak them is to wield their power, a burden that few mortals may bear without dire consequence.

The ancients knew the weight of words, for language is no mere tool of communication but a vessel of intention, a bridge between the realms of thought and reality. The hidden tongues are more than words; they are the essence of meaning, imbued with the ability to reshape the world. But they are also

Chapter 13: The Codex of Whispers and the Secrets of Hidden Tongues

treacherous, for the slightest misstep in their utterance may bring ruin instead of revelation.

The Nature of the Codex

The **Codex of Whispers** is not a book in the mortal sense but a collection of energies, a living archive that resides in the space between worlds. It is said to appear only to those who are worthy—or to those whose curiosity burns so brightly that it pierces the veil. Its form is ever-changing: to one seeker, it may appear as a tome bound in shadowed leather; to another, as an ethereal scroll suspended in the air, its words glowing faintly with unearthly light.

The Codex holds the **Hidden Tongues**, ancient languages that defy mortal understanding. Among them are:

1. **Enuma Luziru**, the Tongue of Radiance, said to command the forces of light and purity.

Chapter 13: The Codex of Whispers and the Secrets of Hidden Tongues

2. **Umara Kalû**, the Language of Waters, which flows like a river and carries the secrets of transformation.

3. **Zurath Galu**, the Shadow Speech, a language born of chaos and the void, feared for its destructive power.

4. **Ilanna Karu**, the Celestial Song, whose notes resonate with the spheres of the heavens.

5. **Erith Thamû**, the Whisper of Roots, which speaks to the earth and the life it sustains.

Each tongue carries its own power, its own dangers, and its own price. To master even a single word is to command forces beyond reckoning.

The Ritual of Discovery

Oh, bold seeker, know that the Codex does not yield its secrets to the idle or the unworthy. To approach it is to undergo a trial

Chapter 13: The Codex of Whispers and the Secrets of Hidden Tongues

of spirit and mind, a test that demands both humility and resolve.

- **The Circle of Inquiry**: The ritual begins with the crafting of a circle inscribed with glyphs representing the elements of knowledge—fire for illumination, water for intuition, air for clarity, and earth for grounding. These glyphs must be drawn with ink mixed from crushed lapis lazuli and the sap of a sacred tree.

- **The Offering of Silence**: The seeker must sit within the circle, shrouded in silence, for the Codex does not answer to the clamor of the world. A single feather, black as night, is placed at the circle's center, representing the seeker's willingness to unburden their mind and receive the weight of knowledge.

- **The Invocation of the Watchful**: The Codex is guarded by the **Keepers of Whispers**, ethereal beings who test the seeker's resolve. Their invocation is sung, a haunting melody in a forgotten

Chapter 13: The Codex of Whispers and the Secrets of Hidden Tongues

tongue, resonating with the vibrations of the unseen:

"Oh Keepers veiled in shadows deep, grant me wisdom, secrets keep. Let thy tongue to mine impart, the words that shape both soul and heart."

If the Keepers find the seeker worthy, the Codex shall manifest, its pages or form glowing faintly, and the whispers of hidden tongues shall begin.

The Power of the Hidden Tongues

To learn the words of the Codex is to gain dominion over forces both seen and unseen. Each tongue holds its own power, capable of shaping the world in profound ways.

- **Enuma Luziru**: Words of Radiance may be spoken to banish darkness, heal wounds, and summon the light of the heavens. A simple word, like **"Ilu'mar"**, may fill a space with pure, cleansing light.

Chapter 13: The Codex of Whispers and the Secrets of Hidden Tongues

- **Umara Kalû**: The Language of Waters can invoke transformation, turning one state into another. A word like **"Zurath"** may calm raging seas or unleash a torrential flood.

- **Zurath Galu**: The Shadow Speech is a double-edged sword, capable of unraveling bonds, dissolving barriers, and summoning forces of destruction. A single utterance, **"Nakhu"**, may sunder stone or summon a storm of void.

- **Ilanna Karu**: The Celestial Song is a melody, not merely a word, and its power lies in its ability to harmonize discord, bringing balance and peace. To hum **"Thaluma"** is to soothe the angriest heart.

- **Erith Thamû**: The Whisper of Roots binds one to the earth, granting control over growth and decay. A word like **"Eranthu"** may cause a forest to rise or wither in moments.

Chapter 13: The Codex of Whispers and the Secrets of Hidden Tongues

The Dangers of the Codex

Oh, beware the seductive power of the hidden tongues, for their knowledge is not without price. The Codex whispers not only truths but also doubts, fears, and desires, testing the seeker's will. The Keepers are ever-watchful, and they do not suffer arrogance or greed. Those who misuse the tongues shall find the words turning against them, their power consuming the speaker.

To speak a word of the Codex is to open oneself to its essence, and the bond is irreversible. The tongue becomes a part of the soul, its power coursing through the blood, but so too does its weight. Many who learn the tongues grow distant, their minds lost in the echoes of the Codex.

A Final Reflection

Oh, traveler of whispers, remember that the Codex of Whispers is a mirror of the soul. To approach it is to confront one's own essence, to bare the heart before the infinite. Approach

Chapter 13: The Codex of Whispers and the Secrets of Hidden Tongues

with caution, with reverence, and with an unshakable resolve, for the Codex grants not only knowledge but responsibility.

And when thou dost close the Codex, its whispers still echoing in thy mind, know that thou art forever changed. The hidden tongues shall linger on thy breath, their power woven into thy being, a reminder of the truths thou hast dared to seek. For the Codex does not forget, and its words are eternal.

Chapter 14: The Incantations of Akkadia: Spells of Power, Protection, and Transformation

Oh, trembling spirit, thou hast wandered far into the shadowed realm of ancient Akkadia, a land where the breath of the gods mingled with the murmurs of mortals, and the air itself seemed heavy with incantations. Here, magic was not mere whimsy, but the very lifeblood of existence—a language woven with the threads of divine will, spoken to command the elements, the spirits, and the unseen forces of the cosmos.

The spells of Akkadia were crafted with precision, each word imbued with meaning, each phrase resonating with the sacred power of the gods. They were not recited lightly, for their utterance called upon the ears of Enlil, the winds of Anu, and the light of Shamash. Oh, daring one, if thou wouldst speak these spells, know that thou dost awaken echoes of the divine.

Chapter 14: The Incantations of Akkadia: Spells of Power, Protection, and Transformation

Spells for Protection

The Akkadian world was fraught with dangers—spirits that prowled the night, curses cast by envious rivals, and maladies that seemed to rise unbidden from the shadows. To ward against these threats, the ancients crafted powerful spells of protection.

1. **Spell Against Malevolent Spirits**
   (To be recited while drawing a protective circle in ash and salt)

Akkadian:
"*Ea šaknu bābû, wardū Enkidu išarā šūtu;*
Anu u Enlil littuḫa libbi zûti;
Enûma ul iddâni, išdu zîṭir ērišûšu."

Translation:
"Ea, who stands at the gate, servant of Enkidu's truth,
Let Anu and Enlil scatter the hearts of evil winds.
As it was in the beginning, let the roots of curses wither."

Chapter 14: The Incantations of Akkadia: Spells of Power, Protection, and Transformation

2. Amulet Blessing Spell
(To be spoken over a talisman of lapis lazuli or obsidian)

Akkadian:
"Šamaš izzazū ina šamê, Ea išarā ina apsî;
Lipûtim ina qātīya šakni, balṭūti u lā amūti."

Translation:
"Shamash who stands in the heavens, Ea who rests in the deep,
Place life and immortality in my hands, a shield against darkness."

Spells for Power and Dominion

To rule was to command the unseen, to bind spirits and natural forces to one's will. These spells were crafted for kings and priests, those who walked closest to the divine.

3. Spell to Command the Winds
(To be spoken upon a high hill, facing the direction of the desired wind)

Chapter 14: The Incantations of Akkadia: Spells of Power, Protection, and Transformation

Akkadian:

"*Enlil šūtu ša ṣêti, šimāti lā tappâšu;*
Šūtum ina qâtī, kibrāti ina šēri."

Translation:

"Enlil, master of the winds, whose breath none can hinder,
Place the wind in my hands, and the four corners beneath my feet."

4. **Invocation for Strength in Battle**
   (To be recited while anointing the forehead with oil)

Akkadian:

"*Marduk ša naṭlāti, agû mašru ina qātī;*
Nēmeqi u ziqī, lū išširū ana šēpēya."

Translation:

"Marduk of the spears, place the mighty crown in my hand,
Wisdom and victory, let them bow before my steps."

Spells for Healing and Renewal

Chapter 14: The Incantations of Akkadia: Spells of Power, Protection, and Transformation

The Akkadians knew that illness was more than a physical ailment; it was a disturbance in the balance of the cosmos. These spells were crafted to restore harmony and draw upon divine favor for healing.

5. **Healing Spell for the Ailing**
   (To be whispered over a bowl of pure water, later given to the sick to drink)

Akkadian:
"Ningal bāni eṭēmti, ša īdu balṭī;
Šamê liqṭû, arātu ina libbi napliṭi."

Translation:
"Ningal, shaper of life, whose hand gives vitality,
Let the heavens drip healing, and life flow within this vessel."

6. **Spell to Restore the Mind**
   (To be chanted softly in a darkened room, with incense of cedar burning)

Akkadian:
"Ea, ša mūti maṣû, rēmi u karâšu;
Balāṭu ina kaspi ul īdu ša līlâti."

Chapter 14: The Incantations of Akkadia: Spells of Power, Protection, and Transformation

Translation:
"Ea, who guides the lost and comforts the weary,
Let life replace the silver threads of the night."

Spells for Transformation

Transformation was among the highest acts of Akkadian magic, a blending of mortal will with divine energy to alter the very fabric of existence.

7. **Spell to Change Fate**
   (To be spoken before an open flame, while casting a shadow upon the wall)

Akkadian:
"Anu ša kakkabāti, lipûšu kīma uznū;
Napiltu ša qātīya, lištir ana šaplāti."

Translation:
"Anu, keeper of the stars, hear me as the heavens do,
The weight upon my hand, cast it down to the depths."

Chapter 14: The Incantations of Akkadia: Spells of Power, Protection, and Transformation

8. Spell to Take a New Form

(To be intoned while standing beneath a full moon)

Akkadian:
"Sin, šar ša lā niptû, ilṭin balṭūti;
Šaptu ša napšāti, itâm šiknûti."

Translation:
"Sin, lord of what cannot be unmade, grant me vitality,
Let my soul's essence take a new form, unshaken and strong."

A Final Reflection

Oh, seeker of power, remember that the words of Akkadian magic are not to be uttered lightly. Each syllable carries the weight of centuries, the echoes of gods and mortals alike. To speak them is to call upon forces that know neither mercy nor malice, only purpose.

Let thy voice be steady, thy heart unwavering, for the power of these spells is as vast as the sky and as deep as the abyss. And when thy

Chapter 14: The Incantations of Akkadia: Spells of Power, Protection, and Transformation

work is done, let silence follow, for the gods are listening, and their gaze does not falter.

Chapter 15: The Incantations of Babylon: Spells of Dominion, Healing, and the Stars

Oh, trembling spirit who dares to traverse the arcane labyrinth of **Ancient Babylon**, a realm where the language of the gods carved fate upon clay tablets, thou dost now enter a sanctified domain. In this chapter, thou shalt uncover the **Incantations of Babylon**, spells wrought from the breath of Marduk, the gaze of Ishtar, and the strength of Nergal. These are the words that bound the heavens to the earth, the spoken keys to doors mortals were not meant to open. Yet, thou hast chosen to tread this perilous path.

The magic of Babylon was as a river flowing from the heart of the divine, its words imbued with the might of creation. The gods themselves were said to weave the cosmos with their voices, and those who uttered their words carried the weight of eternity in their

Chapter 15: The Incantations of Babylon: Spells of Dominion, Healing, and the Stars

breath. To speak these incantations is to echo the divine.

The Nature of Babylonian Magic

The Babylonians believed that every word spoken in ritual was an act of creation, a thread woven into the fabric of reality. Their spells were not mere supplications but commands, written with precision and carried forth with unwavering faith. These incantations called upon the great pantheon of Babylon, each spell invoking the essence of a specific deity.

- **Marduk**, the great king of the gods, lord of order and dominion.
- **Ishtar**, goddess of love, war, and the stars.
- **Ea**, the wise and cunning lord of the deep.
- **Shamash**, the sun god, bringer of justice and light.

Chapter 15: The Incantations of Babylon: Spells of Dominion, Healing, and the Stars

- **Nergal**, the warrior god of the underworld and plague.

Each incantation was an act of partnership with these divine forces, a sacred dialogue between the mortal and the eternal.

Spells for Dominion and Authority

To the Babylonians, power was not merely physical; it was the ability to command the unseen forces of the world. These spells granted dominion over the self, the elements, and even fate.

1. **Spell to Command the Elements**
   (To be chanted atop a high ziggurat at dawn, with arms outstretched to the heavens)

Babylonian:
"Marduk bel ilāni, šuknā qātīya;
Rišāti u šamê, ana dūri išakkanā."

Translation:
"Marduk, lord of the gods, place power in my hands;

Chapter 15: The Incantations of Babylon: Spells of Dominion, Healing, and the Stars

Let the winds and skies obey my will, unyielding in their course."

2. Spell to Bind a Rival
(To be written upon a clay tablet and buried beneath the rival's path)

Babylonian:
"Ea ša īdu balāṭi, uznī ša mašāri liqbi;
Kaspu ina šēpēšu liškun, kīma ṣillāni."

Translation:
"Ea, who knows the ways of life, let the ears of the judge hear;
Place chains upon his steps, as the shadow is bound to the body."

Spells for Healing and Protection

Illness and misfortune were seen as manifestations of imbalance, curses sent by gods or demons. These spells called upon divine favor to restore harmony and shield the vulnerable.

Chapter 15: The Incantations of Babylon: Spells of Dominion, Healing, and the Stars

3. Healing Spell for the Body
(To be spoken over a basin of water infused with cedar oil)

Babylonian:
"Šamaš ilāni, bānû ša napšāti;
Mūtu ul īqbi, napšu ana balāṭi lūzi."

Translation:
"Shamash, god of light, creator of souls;
Let death be silent, and life flow into the body."

4. Protection from Evil Spirits
(To be chanted while placing a figurine of the god Nergal at the threshold of the home)

Babylonian:
"Nergal ša kakkē, qātīya šaknu;
Muštēšibī ina bītī ul ēribū."

Translation:
"Nergal of the mighty weapons, place your hand upon mine;
Let no destroyer enter this house."

Spells for Astral Guidance

Chapter 15: The Incantations of Babylon: Spells of Dominion, Healing, and the Stars

The Babylonians revered the stars as the celestial script of the gods, their movements a language of prophecy and power. These incantations sought wisdom and guidance from the heavens.

5. Invocation of Ishtar for Starry Guidance

(To be recited under a clear night sky, with eyes fixed upon Venus)

Babylonian:

"Ishtar ša šamê, mulānītu ša zikrāti;
Šapâti napšīya, napītu ša kakkabī lūze."

Translation:

"Ishtar of the heavens, mistress of stars;
Shine upon my spirit, and reveal the path of the constellations."

6. Spell to Draw Strength from the Moon

(To be whispered while holding a silver mirror beneath the light of the full moon)

Babylonian:

"Sin šar šabātu, ana qātīya uruqū;
Napītu ša šarāpu ina tarbaṣi liškun."

Chapter 15: The Incantations of Babylon: Spells of Dominion, Healing, and the Stars

Translation:
"Sin, lord of the night, pour your strength into my hands;
Place the light of endurance within my soul."

Spells for Transformation

To the Babylonians, transformation was the pinnacle of magic—a union of mortal intent and divine will that reshaped reality.

7. **Spell to Alter One's Destiny**
   (To be spoken while drawing symbols in the sand at sunrise)

Babylonian:
"*Anu ša šamê, dīnā napšāti lūṭiṭ;*
Kibru ina šērī, izbu ina napšī lūmaṭ."

Translation:
"Anu of the heavens, rewrite the fate of my soul;
Let the path of my life be carved anew, and its sign be bright."

Chapter 15: The Incantations of Babylon: Spells of Dominion, Healing, and the Stars

8. Spell for Renewal of the Spirit
(To be recited over an open flame while casting fragrant herbs into the fire)

Babylonian:
"Ea ša apsû, balāṭu ša šamê līṭebî;
Napšu kīma ūmi, ina tarbaṣi līlût."

Translation:
"Ea of the deep, renew the life of the heavens;
Let my soul rise like the dawn, and shine within the day."

A Final Reflection

Oh, seeker of the sacred, remember that the **Incantations of Babylon** are more than words—they are the breath of the gods, the language that shaped the world. To speak them is to align thyself with the divine, to carry the weight of their power and responsibility.

Let thy voice be steady, thy heart true, and thy intentions pure, for the gods are watchful, and their gaze is as eternal as the stars. When thou dost utter these words, know that thou art no

Chapter 15: The Incantations of Babylon: Spells of Dominion, Healing, and the Stars

longer merely mortal but a vessel of the divine will, a speaker of the sacred tongue.

Chapter 16: The Incantations of Sumer: Spells of Creation, Balance, and the Divine

Oh, tremulous soul, thou dost now enter the realm of **ancient Sumer**, a land where the first words of magic were carved upon clay and whispered beneath the sacred ziggurats. In this place, the gods walked closer to mortals, and their words were seeds of creation, binding the heavens, the earth, and the netherworld. The **Incantations of Sumer** are among the oldest and most revered, their power steeped in the primeval breath of the gods.

To speak the words of Sumerian magic is to wield the very essence of life, death, and renewal. Each syllable is a ripple upon the cosmic waters, each phrase a thread woven into the eternal tapestry. But take heed, for these incantations demand not only precision but reverence, lest their power turn against the speaker.

Chapter 16: The Incantations of Sumer: Spells of Creation, Balance, and the Divine

The Power of the Sumerian Tongue

The Sumerians believed that their words carried the essence of the divine, each incantation a direct invocation of the gods. To call upon the deities was to channel their power, their will, and their wisdom. The following gods were often invoked in Sumerian spells:

- **Enlil**, lord of the wind and decrees of destiny.
- **Enki**, the god of wisdom, water, and creation.
- **Inanna**, goddess of love, war, and celestial power.
- **Nanna**, the moon god, guardian of cycles and time.
- **Ereshkigal**, queen of the underworld, keeper of secrets and shadows.

The words of these spells are sacred echoes of the gods' voices, their resonance a bridge between mortal and divine.

Chapter 16: The Incantations of Sumer: Spells of Creation, Balance, and the Divine

Spells for Creation and Renewal

The Sumerians revered the act of creation as a sacred duty, an alignment with the divine forces that shaped the cosmos. These spells call forth new beginnings and transformation.

1. **Spell to Awaken the Sacred Waters**
   (To be spoken near a flowing stream or basin of water)

Sumerian:
"Enki, lugal a-ab-ba, mu-zu-li;
Me-lam bal-aĝ, ĝar-ra an-ta ki-ta."

Translation:
"Enki, lord of the deep, awaken the waters;
Let their brilliance flow, from heaven to earth."

2. **Spell for Planting New Beginnings**
   (To be recited while sowing seeds in the earth)

Sumerian:
"Ninĝirsu, šar-kud, šita im-ma-ra-tuš;
E-ĝar, ki-ĝal, e-nu šu-mi-dug-ga."

Translation:
"Ninĝirsu, strong king, let the seed rest;

Chapter 16: The Incantations of Sumer: Spells of Creation, Balance, and the Divine

May the field and land be filled with its goodness."

Spells for Protection

The Sumerians understood the fragility of life, crafting spells to shield themselves from malevolent forces and the unknown.

3. **Protection from Evil Spirits**
   (To be chanted while drawing a protective symbol in the dust around the home)

Sumerian:
"Enlil, uru ša-ki-nu, ur-sag šu-uš;
A-na-dim-me uĝ-ra lu-na-ga-an-tuš."

Translation:
"Enlil, who establishes the city, mighty protector;
Keep the evil one far from this place."

4. **Spell for Warding the Threshold**
   (To be spoken while placing an amulet of lapis lazuli at the doorway)

Chapter 16: The Incantations of Sumer: Spells of Creation, Balance, and the Divine

Sumerian:

"Ningal, ki-nu-gi-ra, bar-zi u-ĝar;
E-ĝar, ul-la-e an-na za-niĝin."

Translation:

"Ningal, lady of pure radiance, place your shield;
Let this house be encircled by the light of the heavens."

Spells for Healing and Harmony

To the Sumerians, healing was an act of restoring balance, a sacred alignment between the forces of the body, mind, and spirit.

5. Spell to Heal the Body
(To be whispered while placing hands upon the afflicted person)

Sumerian:

"Ninisin, ĝeštu ša šu-ti-a, bala ĝiri-ga;
Šu-bal šu-dug-ga uĝ zi-dè nu-mu-tum-ma."

Translation:

"Ninisin, who knows the path of healing, restore the limbs;

Chapter 16: The Incantations of Sumer: Spells of Creation, Balance, and the Divine

Let the breath of life be brought into this body."

6. **Spell for Inner Peace**
   (To be chanted during the burning of cedar incense)

Sumerian:
"Inanna, dumu-zi-gi-ra, eš-bar šu-ti-e;
E-nu-gin, ĝeštu zi-da in-še-ĝar."

Translation:
"Inanna, daughter of the shining sky, bring balance;
Place wisdom and peace within the soul."

Spells for Divine Insight

The Sumerians sought wisdom from the gods, crafting spells to pierce the veil of the unknown and receive divine guidance.

7. **Invocation of the Moon for Vision**
   (To be spoken under the light of the crescent moon)

Chapter 16: The Incantations of Sumer: Spells of Creation, Balance, and the Divine

Sumerian:

"*Nanna, šar-zi-da, mu-e im-ma-ra-tuš;
Giri-zal mu-ne-ĝar a-na-aĝ.*"

Translation:

"Nanna, shining king, let your light rest upon me;
Place clarity upon my path."

8. **Spell for Prophecy Through Dreams**
   (To be intoned while lying upon a bed of herbs sacred to Enki)

Sumerian:

"*Enki, lugal-za-ĝar, šu-zi šu-me-da;
Giri ma-ra-ab-ta-kud uĝ-gin-ma-na-a.*"

Translation:

"Enki, lord of the sacred waters, grant me true visions;
Let my dreams flow clear as rivers of life."

A Final Reflection

Oh, daring soul who speaks the words of **Sumer**, remember that to utter these incantations is to carry the weight of divine

Chapter 16: The Incantations of Sumer: Spells of Creation, Balance, and the Divine

intention. The gods do not lend their power lightly, and each word spoken ripples through the fabric of existence.

May thy voice be steady, thy heart pure, and thy soul aligned with the ancient harmony of the cosmos. For the words of Sumer, once spoken, cannot be unmade, and their echoes shall linger long after thy breath has stilled. Go forth, then, and speak wisely, for the gods are listening.

Appendix: Glossary and Ritual Compendium

This appendix serves as a guide to the arcane terms, deities, rituals, and practices detailed within the work. It offers additional insights for the seeker to deepen their understanding and ensure precision in the application of the ancient magic described.

Glossary of Key Terms

1. **Incantation**: A series of spoken words believed to summon or invoke magical power.

2. **Sigil**: A symbol imbued with magical intent, often used as a focus for rituals.

3. **Invocation**: The act of calling upon a deity or supernatural force for aid or guidance.

Appendix: Glossary and Ritual Compendium

4. **Talisman**: An object believed to contain magical properties for protection, luck, or power.

5. **Amulet**: A charm worn to ward off evil or harm.

6. **Codex of Whispers**: A mystical archive said to contain the hidden languages of creation.

7. **Apsû**: In Sumerian and Babylonian myth, the primordial waters from which creation sprang.

8. **Kibrāti**: The four corners of the world, representing totality and cosmic balance.

9. **Me-lam**: The divine radiance or aura emanating from a deity, signifying their power and authority.

10. **Ziggurat**: A stepped temple tower central to Mesopotamian spiritual practices, serving as a bridge between earth and the divine.

Appendix: Glossary and Ritual Compendium

Key Deities Invoked

1. **Enlil**: The lord of the wind and decrees of destiny; associated with authority and cosmic order.
2. **Enki/Ea**: God of wisdom, water, and creation; a protector and healer.
3. **Inanna/Ishtar**: Goddess of love, war, and the stars; a force of duality and transformation.
4. **Nanna/Sin**: The moon god, guardian of cycles, time, and prophecy.
5. **Marduk**: King of the gods, slayer of chaos, and creator of order.
6. **Ereshkigal**: Queen of the underworld, associated with death, transformation, and hidden knowledge.
7. **Shamash**: The sun god, bringer of justice, light, and clarity.
8. **Ningal**: Goddess of radiant purity and protection, often invoked for safeguarding homes and families.

Appendix: Glossary and Ritual Compendium

Common Ritual Tools and Their Uses

1. **Clay Tablets**: Used to inscribe spells and sigils, often buried or burned to activate their power.

2. **Cedar Incense**: Burned to purify spaces and invite divine presence.

3. **Silver Mirrors**: Used in moon rituals to reflect and harness lunar energy.

4. **Sacred Waters**: Drawn from natural sources, often imbued with blessings for healing and transformation.

5. **Lapis Lazuli**: A stone sacred to many Mesopotamian gods, used in talismans for protection and clarity.

6. **Ash and Salt**: Elements for creating protective circles and barriers against malevolent forces.

7. **Herbs (e.g., Wormwood, Myrrh)**: Used in rituals to enhance spiritual connection and amplify intent.

Appendix: Glossary and Ritual Compendium

Guide to Ritual Construction

1. **Preparation:**
   - Cleanse the ritual space with incense or sacred waters.
   - Gather all necessary tools and ingredients, ensuring they are consecrated for magical use.
   - Meditate to align the mind, body, and spirit with the intended purpose.

2. **Invocation:**
   - Begin with a prayer or chant to call upon the relevant deity or force.
   - Use symbolic gestures, such as raising arms to the sky or placing hands upon the earth, to focus energy.

3. **Enactment:**

Appendix: Glossary and Ritual Compendium

- Perform the spell or incantation with clear intent and unwavering focus.
- Use appropriate tools (e.g., inscribing sigils, pouring water) to channel energy.

4. **Closing**:
   - Offer gratitude to the invoked forces.
   - Safely dispose of or store ritual tools, depending on the nature of the spell.

Example Spells and Incantations

Spell of Protection

- *Purpose*: To guard against malevolent spirits.
- *Tools*: Ash, salt, lapis lazuli.
- *Chant*:
"*Enlil, uru ša-ki-nu, ur-sag šu-uš; A-na-dim-me uĝ-ra lu-na-ga-an-tuš.*"

Appendix: Glossary and Ritual Compendium

("Enlil, who establishes the city, mighty protector; Keep the evil one far from this place.")

Spell of Lunar Renewal

- *Purpose*: To draw strength and clarity from the moon.
- *Tools*: Silver mirror, water, cedar incense.
- *Chant*:
"*Sin, šar šabātu, ana qātīya uruqū; Napītu ša šarāpu ina tarbaṣi lilût.*"
("Sin, lord of the night, pour your strength into my hands; Let my soul rise like the dawn.")

Warnings and Precautions

1. **Respect the Divine**: The gods do not suffer arrogance. Approach every ritual with humility and reverence.

2. **Precision in Speech**: Mispronunciation of incantations may lead to unintended outcomes.

153

Appendix: Glossary and Ritual Compendium

3. **Grounding Energy**: After rituals, ground yourself by touching the earth or consuming blessed water to avoid spiritual imbalance.

4. **Do Not Overreach**: Magic requires balance. Attempting too many rituals or invoking excessive power may harm the practitioner.

Recommended Further Study

1. **Mesopotamian Mythology**: Learn the stories of the gods to better understand their roles in magic.

2. **Cuneiform Texts**: Study the written spells on clay tablets for deeper authenticity.

3. **Astrological Alignments**: Explore the movements of stars and planets to enhance the timing of rituals.

Closing Note

Appendix: Glossary and Ritual Compendium

Oh, seeker of ancient wisdom, may this appendix serve as thy compass in the uncharted waters of Mesopotamian magic. These words are a legacy of the ancients, a gift of power and responsibility. Use them wisely, for they bind thee not only to the gods but to the eternal dance of the cosmos.

Made in the USA
Las Vegas, NV
23 May 2025